Digital War Reporting

DONALD MATHESON
AND
STUART ALLAN

polity

First published in 2009 by Polity Press

Polity Press
65 Bridge Street
Cambridge CB2 1UR, UK

Polity Press
350 Main Street
Malden, MA 02148, USA

ISBN-13: 978-0-7456-4275-8
ISBN-13: 978-0-7456-4276-5 (pb)

A catalogue record for this book is available from the British Library.

Typeset in 10.25 on 13 pt FF Scala
by Servis Filmsetting Ltd, Stockport, Cheshire
Printed and bound by the MPG Books Group, UK

The publisher has used its best endeavours to ensure that the URLs for external websites referred to in this book are correct and active at the time of going to press. However, the publisher has no responsibility for the websites and can make no guarantee that a site will remain live or that the content is or will remain appropriate.

For further information on Polity, visit our website: www.politybooks.com

Contents

CHAPTER ONE

New Wars, New Reporting

Introduction

The carpet of the mosque is stained with blood and covered with fragments of concrete. Tank shells and machine-gun rounds have pitted the inside walls. The rotting, sweet smell of death hangs in the morning air. Gunsmoke-laced sunbeams illuminate the bodies of four Iraqi insurgents. A fifth lies next to a column, his entire body covered by a blanket.

I shudder. Something very wrong has happened here.

(Sites, 2007: 5)

These words, written by Kevin Sites, a freelance correspondent for NBC News at the time, open his account of events that transpired in a mosque in Falluja, Iraq, on 13 November 2004. Sites, 'embedded' with the United States Third Battalion, First Marine Regiment, proceeds to explain what happened next. One member of the regiment, a lance corporal, observes that one of the Iraqi insurgents, lying motionless on the ground at his feet, is still breathing. Sites, videotaping the scene, continues:

I see him [the lance corporal] in my viewfinder; he is raising his M-16 rifle and pointing it directly at the wounded insurgent's head. He peers down at him through his laser scope.

I don't know what he's going to do, but I hope he's just going to cover him while other Marines search him for weapons. But in this place, already filled with so much death, somehow, in this moment, I sense there will be more. The lance corporal squeezes the trigger, firing a 5.62 round into the man's head, which I watch explode on my screen.

His skull and brains splatter against the dirty white wall he was lying against. After the shot, the Marine (whom I have

chosen not to name) turns on his heels and walks away. (Ibid.:
13)

Bearing witness to people being killed in combat was nothing new to Sites, a seasoned war reporter, but 'never like this.
Never at point-blank range', he adds. His camera still rolling, he
promptly completes the sequence, stunned by what he has seen.
Then, when it looks like a fifth wounded Iraqi is about to be shot
dead, he intervenes to confront the Marine who had pulled the
trigger.

> 'Why did you do that?' I asked him. 'What's going on? These
> were the same guys that were here yesterday. They were
> wounded.'
> 'I didn't know, sir,' he said. 'I didn't know.' The voice that had
> seemed so confident just a few moments ago is now filled with
> unsettling realizations. And then he walks out of the mosque
> followed by the other Marines. (Ibid.: 14)

Sites left the mosque shortly thereafter – leaving behind the fifth
man – to travel back to the battalion field headquarters. He was
determined to tell the Lieutenant Colonel in charge what had
happened and to show him the videotape. In choosing to leave
the wounded man behind, however, Sites was making a decision
that he would profoundly regret. Later he learned, from an official report obtained using the Freedom of Information Act, that
the man 'had been shot twenty-three times after I left. Almost
all of the entry wounds were in his back – execution style' (ibid.:
289). The report's ballistic evidence would leave little doubt in
Sites's mind that 'a Marine or Marines killed the only living Iraqi
witness to all that had occurred inside that mosque' (ibid.: 290).

The reason Sites had been in the Falluja mosque that day was
due, in part, to his particular skills in making the most of the
digital technology available to him. He filed his stories to a computer server in the US using a laptop and a telephone book-sized
RBGAN (Regional Broadband Global Area Network) satellite
modem. Video was sent via FTP (File Transfer Protocol), which
few journalists with rival networks knew how to do. 'Technology',

Embedded with US Marines in Iraq and using lightweight digital video gear, freelance journalist Kevin Sites records the killing of an unarmed wounded man in a Falluja mosque (November 2004). © Rex Features

he later recalled, 'had shrunk the world to a much more manageable size just in time for this battle' in Falluja (Sites, 2007: 13). Moreover, his presence was also attributable to the way he had handled his role as an embedded journalist, having worked hard to establish a good relationship with his unit. The Marines, he felt, respected his self-reliance – that is, the fact that he shot, wrote and transmitted his reports without a crew. They also appreciated his independent weblog (permitted by NBC because of his freelance status) on the internet. In addition to sharing in-depth personal stories of his experiences, Sites had been posting digital photographs of Marines for the benefit of their families back home. Following the broadcast of his videotape of what happened in Falluja that day, however, the messages of gratitude from the families would be replaced by a torrent of hate mail, including death threats.

In dealing with what he described as 'the most soul-wrenching moral dilemma I have ever faced in my life', Sites alerted NBC to his videotape and the incident it documented, knowing that its eventual broadcast would be certain to have far-reaching consequences. 'My professional code of ethics commands me to "seek and report the truth"', he maintained, 'but it also, as few outside the profession know, instructs us to "minimize harm"' (Sites, 2007: 15). There was every possibility, he feared, that, once word of the video reached the insurgents, they would be less willing to surrender to US troops. Moreover, its release risked further inflaming the insurgency, leading to even more violence – including with regard to the treatment of coalition prisoners. Consequently, in weighing up his professional responsibility in relation to a consideration of the potential harm the material might engender, he and his NBC News colleagues (among them executive and senior producers, as well as lawyers) agonized over what was the right course of action. In the end, it was decided that two versions of the video would be released. One feed would be the full version, while the second would be an edited treatment, pausing at the moment when the Marine raised his rifle to point at the insurgent's head. It was this version that was eventually broadcast by NBC, which Sites realized, in retrospect, was a mistake. Although he himself had pushed for this decision – believing that self-censorship could be justified on the basis that the images were too graphic for viewers – it quickly became apparent that it meant audiences would be unable to understand precisely what had happened. 'Because they didn't get the whole story', he explained, 'viewers filled their lack of understanding with their own conclusions, based on personal perceptions, political beliefs and emotional reactions – almost anything but factual detail. The very thing we held back on' (ibid.: 18). Not surprisingly, Sites surmised, many viewers concluded that the Marine was justified in what he had done.

During the broadcast, NBC News anchor Brian Williams, in what Sites considered to be 'an incredibly generous gesture to me and the burgeoning blog movement', mentioned that Sites maintained an independent war weblog (hereafter blog). 'He then read the Internet address on air to his ten million viewers', Sites recalled, 'inadvertently sending thousands of rabid right-wingers to my electronic front door' (2007: 19). Connecting his laptop to the satellite modem the next morning in Falluja, he discovered more than 600 e-mails waiting to be read, with more to follow at a staggering rate for the next year (due, in large part, to right-wing bloggers and the conservative Fox News channel fanning the flames of controversy). In realizing that all of the other US news networks had followed NBC's decision not to show the actual shooting in the video, he recognized that the self-censorship had proven chillingly effective. This stood in marked contrast to newscasts broadcast elsewhere, many of which had shown the incident in its entirety (repeatedly, in the case of Al Jazeera, for example). 'Everyone in the world had the potential to see one of the most important and controversial stories to come out the war – except the citizens of the nation whose own military was directly involved', Sites observed (ibid.: 23).

Sites's response was to turn to his warblog, knowing that it afforded him the only means to place his unedited version of the story on the public record. On 21 November 2004, eight days after the incident, he posted an 'Open letter to the Devil Dogs of the 3.1' explaining his actions directly to the Marines concerned. Its final two paragraphs state:

> So here, ultimately, is how it plays out: When the Iraqi man in the mosque posed a threat, he was your enemy; when he was subdued, he was your responsibility; when he was killed in front of my eyes and my camera, the story of his death became my responsibility.
>
> The burdens of war, as you so well know, are unforgiving for all of us. (Sites, 2007: 25–6)

The response to the blog posting was astonishing, with excerpts of the letter carried in news reports around the globe. Sites's readership statistics, having been registering around 37,600 earlier in the month, leapt to more than 2 million the day following the post. Although the hate mail would continue for some time, he quickly became convinced that he was seeing 'the trend of hate shift either to begrudging understanding of my actions or outright support now that more information is available' (ibid.: 26). His blog, he believed, had engendered a remarkable impact on the perceptions of the US public.

This example raises a number of important questions about contemporary war journalism that will prove to be central to the discussion unfolding throughout this book. Our emphasis will be on the ways reporters – professionals and ordinary citizens alike – narrativize the exigencies of conflict – that is, how they bear witness to the horrors around them. As this description of Sites's experience illustrates, emerging technologies have made different kinds of reporting possible and placed those who produce such accounts in new relationships with others, near and distant. Few reporters were present in Falluja during the US assault on the insurgent stronghold in November 2004 for a range of reasons discussed later in the book, and it is likely, although of course impossible to know with any certainty, that this footage would not have emerged without the combination of Sites's digital equipment, his skills in using it and his commitment to extend the boundaries of reporting. The result was not in any simple sense the independence that many journalists expect to find in new technology (discussed further shortly). For the technology placed him in closer contact with editors, whose response to the video of the shooting of wounded prisoners was inevitably different to his own. It also tightened still further the feedback loop between the production of news and its audiences' responses, thereby intensifying the purchase of ethical responsibilities on the war correspondent while simultaneously taking away the time to think. Sites's discovery of the power of personal media – a discovery echoed in a diverse array of contexts in the pages that follow – to carve out a space to tell his story of war outside the confines of 'traditional' conventions introduced further complexities. Suddenly, he was free to try to correct the editing decision he saw as wrong; yet he also became vulnerable to personal attack. At the same moment, both the reporter, now distinct from the news organization, and the audience, newly empowered by – and sometimes vociferous in its use of – the interactive media of e-mail and the web, came to the fore, providing an entirely new space of reporting with significant consequences for what was covered, how and why. It is thus readily apparent that emerging digital technologies will not resolve long-standing struggles over the representation of war, but rather will pose them in new, challenging ways.

In tracing the journalistic uses of technology, and the political and ethical tensions which recurrently arise as a consequence, this book re-examines familiar assumptions about war reporting from a unique vantage point. Allan and Zelizer (2004: 4) note that war reporting often functions as a kind of 'litmus test' for journalism, as its daunting circumstances throw into sharp relief existing criteria of good journalism, such as impartiality, fairness or even an alignment with a 'national interest'. Extraordinary demands are placed on journalism, demands which can sometimes elude even the most conscientious of reporters. It is our hope that this book's exploration of the forms and practices of digital war reporting will engender a fresh perspective into the harsh realities of the reporting process while, at the same time, contributing to current debates about journalism's role in shaping public perceptions of the nature of warfare itself.

The rapidity of change unfolding across the media landscape is a central theme of the book. In considering the ongoing war in Iraq, for example, one would be forgiven for thinking that the innovations heralded during the first Gulf War in 1990–1 now seem strangely antiquated. 'The big difference is that in '91 everything was analog and now everything is digital', observed Dick Tauber, vice president of satellites and circuits for CNN, in 2003. 'Back then, a satellite transponder could send a single video and audio channel to a satellite and back to headquarters. Now we can send half a dozen channels in the same amount of space.' Moreover, equipment had become smaller, lighter and more robust. Journalists wanting to do a stand-up report to camera, but unable to use a videophone, were able to press mini-portable television stations, called 'fly-aways', into service. 'In the first Gulf War, the fly-away was stowed in 30 cases, the size of luggage, and weighed a ton', Tauber recalled. 'Now it's in 10 or 12 cases the size of a laptop and weighs much less' (cited in Megna, 2003). Insistent claims that technological progress necessarily improves the quality of journalism circulate widely, many of which revolve around the constant struggle to get the story through. In 1991 in Baghdad, the likes of CNN's Peter Arnett opened up modes of reporting where journalism appeared to sidestep the censors: he engaged in live, unrehearsed question-and-answer sessions with the news channel's anchors. Dowell (2005) cites the story of a US reporter imprisoned by the Indonesian government while reporting on the last stages of the independence struggle in Timor Leste in 1999, who was able to continue broadcasting on the complicity of Indonesian troops in the atrocities against Timorese using his video-enabled cell phone.

Still, such descriptions of how emerging technologies can empower journalism with greater freedom require careful quali-fication in light of countervailing pressures. Deibert (2008) is one of many scholars to express disquiet about how quickly powerful political actors seek to recuperate digital media to their field of control. He charts growing surveillance, censorship and legal restrictions in a range of countries on the internet, a trend reinforced – and ostensibly legitimized in the eyes of some – in the wake of the Al Qaeda attacks on September 11, 2001. Similarly, Seib (2004: 47) suggests that the US military actively encouraged journalists such as Sites to 'embed' with troops in Iraq as part of their attempts to control the 'unprecedented inde-pendence' that real-time communication had given journalists. Embedding, with its promise of live coverage from the front line, brought the media within military-devised codes of conduct. At the same time, the internet, while a space where reporters such as Sites could tell their own version of events, was also a place characterized by a reduced respect for journalistic authority.

This book thus strives to offer a critical appraisal of the relative technological affordances and limitations engendered by digital war reporting. It will detail the convergence of media processes that has allowed reporters on the front lines to relay video footage to their editors back in the newsroom and has enabled citizens equipped with a cell or mobile phone to adopt the role of a journalist in the event that they find themselves in the wrong place at the wrong time. It will discuss the compression of the lived dynamics of time, space and place which result from the ever-increasing capacity of digital communications networks to rewrite the geopolitics of information. It will examine the rise of personal media in wartime, produced by individuals from correspondents to soldiers and civilians, challenging the power of major news organizations to set the agenda. At the same time, in order to assess the digital mediation of warfare, technological innovation must be situated in the wider context of journalism's representational forms, practices and epistemologies. Rather than 'digital media' being studied as if they existed outside of wider social contexts, they must be approached in light of the communicative dynamics they engender, transform and resist.

In the remainder of this chapter, we begin this process of contextualization by opening up for exploration pressing questions about the status of digital war reporting and its truth-telling power.

War in a digital age

A common thread in the reflections of many commentators concerned with how war is represented is the recognition that the categories of warfare and mediation are becoming increasingly difficult to separate from one another. While observers such as Knightley (2004) describe a struggle within news journalism to maintain some independence from official versions of war, others have taken the argument a step further to regard the media as an integral part of military and political campaigns to wage war in the first place. Regardless of journalists' aspirations to give impartial accounts of conflict, Payne (2005) argues, governments need to win the battle for domestic (and, to a lesser extent, international) public opinion. This necessarily revolves around a need to gain international legitimacy for the conduct of war, requiring that they co-opt the media as part of the 'information' (or propaganda, in the eyes of some) initiatives that precede hostilities. Others note that military strategy relies increasingly upon control of the information space of war – from surveillance technologies which can pinpoint targets to psychological operations (PSYOP) campaigns intended to demoralize the enemy. As this book was readied for publication in early 2009, Israel's aerial and ground attack on Hamas in the Palestinian territory of Gaza involved, among its first actions, the bombing of the Gazan television station Al Aqsa and the banning of foreign journalists from entering the territory. While people have for a long time died for a pennant or what was painted on a coat of arms, in Virilio's (1989: 85) phrase, the status of media technologies as a military target in their own right has somehow pushed the realm of the symbolic into a new prominence in the conduct of war.

Indeed, the capacity of the media to shape public perceptions now figures increasingly prominently in scholarly accounts of the nature of warfare itself. Voices from within the military and strategic communities are heralding the astonishing speed of change in war-fighting tactics, many of which have been ushered in by advances in digital computers and related types of communications hardware. Notions of command and control (C^2), coupled with intelligence (C^2I), have been extended to encompass first communications (C^3) and now computers (C^4) when the ability of military commanders to co-ordinate their forces is being assessed. Similarly, bold claims made about 'cyberwar' often invoke the military concept of Revolution in Military Affairs (RMA) as a means to explain how the character and conduct of military operations are evolving. Singled out for attention are the technological imperatives engendering these changes, especially with regard to globalized security networks, so as better to anticipate how warfare will be waged in future. The capacity of new innovations in 'info-tech' to rewrite the rules of strategic doctrine

may be widely recognized, but in the meantime contrary sce-
narios regarding how superiority is to be achieved on the 'digital
battlefield' continue to multiply.

Central in this endeavour is the increasing sophistication of
the tactics of 'perception management', a trend which cannot be
understood without paying attention to tensions between journalism and the military dating from the early 1990s. At the time of
the US-led intervention in Kosovo, the subject of our next chapter, military officials were striving to recast the military–media
relationship in light of the lessons learned from the decade's earlier conflicts, beginning with the Gulf War of 1991. The advent of
rolling 24-hour 'real-time' global television news services, with
CNN leading the way, had helped to transform the conflict into
a media spectacle akin to a video game. Largely displaced by this
'Nintendo effect', critics pointed out, were the consequences of
war – that is, the horrific loss of human life. In the words of veteran war correspondent Chris Hedges: 'The Gulf War made war
fashionable again. It was a cause the nation willingly embraced.
It gave us media-manufactured heroes and a heady pride in our
military superiority and technology. It made war fun' (2002:
142–3). The blame for this type of reporting, he argues, rests on
the shoulders of the press for co-operating so closely with the
military:

> Television reporters happily disseminated the spoon-fed images
> that served the propaganda effort of the military and the state.
> These images did little to convey the reality of war. Pool report-
> ers, those guided around in groups by the military, wrote about
> 'our boys' eating packaged army food, practicing for chemical
> weapons attacks, and bathing out of buckets in the desert. It was
> war as spectacle, war as entertainment. The images and stories
> were designed to make us feel good about our nation, about
> ourselves. The Iraqi families and soldiers being blown to bits
> by huge iron fragmentation bombs just over the border in Iraq
> were faceless and nameless phantoms. (Ibid.: 143)

There is little doubt that the ensuing 'sanitized' news coverage
succeeded in profound ways in shaping how media audiences

perceived the nature of a 'clean war' waged with 'pinpoint accuracy'. News management in the Gulf War, Knightley concurs, had at its core 'a deliberate attempt by the authorities to alter public perception of the nature of war itself, particularly the fact that civilians die in war' (1991: 5; see also Cumings, 1992; Jeffords and Rabinovitz, 1994; Keeble, 1997; Kellner, 2004; Reese, 2004; Taylor, 1992).

Sanitized news coverage, critics pointed out, was certain to produce desensitized audiences, passively observing each development in the 'video game war' with little regard to its implications (the contrast with Vietnam, the 'living room war', being all too telling). Journalistic efforts to enhance public understanding, to counter this obsession with immediacy with rigorous, in-depth reports offering interpretation and context, were being increasingly frustrated. Throughout the 1990s, Western news organizations were rationalized in the name of cost savings, their budgets for international newsgathering slashed dramatically as economic pressures were brought to bear. The gradual thawing of the Cold War was a further factor, seemingly providing justification for what became a dramatic reallocation of resources away from specialized military reporting (freelancers became the norm as travel budgets were cut and foreign bureaus closed) in favour of more 'popular' (and 'efficient' – i.e. inexpensive) news stories. Some news executives insisted this was simply giving the public what it wanted, pointing to declining viewing (and newspaper circulation) figures as evidence that international news could not attract the necessary advertising revenues to satisfy 'bottom-line' calculations. Less debatable was the fact that owners were increasingly seeing news as a commodity, with some forms of it more profitable than others regardless of accompanying claims made about public service.

Peter Arnett, a household name for his reports for CNN during the Gulf War (he was the only Western television correspondent in Baghdad for much of the conflict), was one of several leading journalists to express his discontent publicly at the time. International news coverage in the mainstream US press, he

argued, had 'almost reached the vanishing point' since the conflict in the Gulf earlier in the decade:

> Today, a foreign story that doesn't involve bombs, natural dis-
> asters or financial calamity has little chance of entering the
> American consciousness. This at a time when the United
> States has become the world's lone superpower and 'news' has
> so many venues – papers, magazines, broadcast and cable TV,
> radio, newsletters, the Internet – that it seems inescapable. So
> how is it that Americans have never been less informed about
> what's going on in the rest of the world? Because we, the media,
> have stopped telling them. (Arnett, 1998)

Far too many editors had simply embraced 'the canard that
readers don't want foreign news', he maintained, even though
contrary evidence was available, not least public opinion surveys.
Meanwhile more upbeat assessments pointed to how CNN, in
pioneering the concept of 'news on demand', had demonstrated
that there was public enthusiasm for such stories so long as they
were presented in ways that heightened liveness and immediacy.
The trick, advocates of the emergent digital technologies believed,
was to make the most of the 'new generation' of news-gathering
strategies promising to revolutionize war reporting.

For a number of scholars working at the interface of international relations and media technology, further questions need
to be posed about the very dynamics of mediation influencing
public perceptions. James Der Derian (2001, 2004) contends
that the distanced and one-sided representations of war on television have emerged within a political reconceptualization of
war to Western publics as bloodless and virtuous. 'Technology in
the service of virtue has given rise to a global form of virtual violence', he contends, namely 'virtuous war' (Der Derian, 2001: xi).
In coining this term, which he acknowledges sounds like a 'felic-
itous oxymoron', it is his intention to underscore the tensions
between 'people who believe you can use war to achieve ethical
aims – that's the virtue part of it – and the virtual, how you can
fight wars now from a remote distance and have minimal casualties, on your own side' (Der Derian, 2004). The danger at the

heart of this contradiction, it follows, is the implied belief that military violence is the most effective means to resolve seemingly intractable political problems. 'If you have the technological superiority, and you believe in your ethical superiority, these factors combine to a very nasty effect', he adds. More likely than not 'you defer civilian diplomatic action and give the military the opportunity to step into this vacuum and offer up solutions' (ibid.).

In advancing this thesis, Der Derian is maintaining that virtuous war evolved from the United States' rationale for deploying battlefield technologies in the first Gulf War and its aerial campaigns in Bosnia and Kosovo. Technical capability was aligned with a declared ethical imperative to actualize violence from a distance with minimal casualties to US forces. 'Using networked information and virtual technologies to bring "there" here in near-real time and with near-verisimilitude', Der Derian writes, 'virtuous war exercises a comparative as well as strategic advantage for the digitally advanced' (2001: xv). To wage virtuous war is to make every effort to remove from sight the victims of the violence perpetrated from afar:

> On the surface, virtuous war cleans up the political discourse as well as the battlefield. Fought in the same manner as they are represented, by real-time surveillance and TV 'live-feeds,' virtuous wars promote a vision of bloodless, humanitarian, hygienic wars. We can rattle off casualty rates of prototypical virtuous conflicts like the Gulf War (270 Americans lost their lives – more than half in accidents), the Mogadishu raid (eighteen Americans killed), and the Kosovo air campaign (barring accidents, a remarkable zero casualty conflict for the NATO forces). Yet most of us would not know the casualty figures for the other side, of Iraqis, Somalis, and Serbs. Post-Vietnam, the US has made many digital advances; public announcement of enemy body counts is not one of them. (Der Derian, 2001: xv)

Virtuous war, in other words, exploits digital technologies to project an ethos of killing in sharp contrast with previous forms of warfare. Fact blurs with fiction as virtuality collapses reality into computer simulations, thereby obscuring who is responsible – and thus to be held accountable – for killing others (for whom virtuous war is no less devastating in its horrors than any other type of war). 'One experiences "death" but not the tragic consequences of it', Der Derian writes. 'In virtuous war we now face not just the confusion but the pixilation of war and game on the same screen' (ibid.: xvi).

To suggest that the advent of digital technologies has recast familiar distinctions between 'old' and 'new' wars is to open up for debate a number of intriguing issues. This distinction has been theorized by Mary Kaldor (2003, 2006), who offers an insightful assessment of its conceptual implications for thinking anew about warfare in a post-Cold War context. Briefly, in discerning what is new about 'new' wars, she proceeds to argue that their emergence is contingent upon various – often informal, even inchoate – networks which advocate exclusivist causes (diaspora groups, for example, often come to the fore in this regard). Moreover, new wars typically bring to bear an array of global actors, while tending to be 'concentrated in areas where the modern state is unravelling and where the distinctions between internal and external, public and private, no longer have the same meaning' as they did in 'old' wars (Kaldor, 2003: 120).

Two dimensions of this kind of warfare are particularly relevant for this book, with its emphasis upon wars directly involving Western governments. On the one hand, Kaldor describes the emergence of a similar conceptualization to that described by Der Derian. 'Spectacle warfare', primarily a form of war conducted by the US, first in the Gulf War, is war at a distance, fought through air sorties or proxies such as the Afghanistan Northern Alliance. Like Der Derian, Kaldor notes both the extent to which these wars are projected to audiences as free of (Western) casualties and, indeed, their symbolic nature. This concept 'emphasizes the function of war as a form of political legitimation, an ideology, in a context where citizens are no longer ready to sacrifice their lives and governments are no longer ready to guarantee the full range of rights' (2003: 126). On the other hand, she locates new wars

in conditions where failed or failing states have lost their claim
to legitimacy, usually on account of declining economies (and
thereby collapsing investment, production, and taxation) and
increased corruption. Structural inequalities, including where
unemployment and rural–urban migration are concerned, soon
become entrenched in a manner likely to weaken the rule of law.
Here, 'network warfare' emerges, conducted by armed networks
of state and non-state actors, such as units of regular forces (or
other security forces), as well as paramilitary groups, charismatic
warlords, terrorist cells, religious fundamentalists, organized
criminal groups, mercenaries, and so forth. War is, for these
actors, a form of political mobilization, Kaldor contends, where
'the point of violence is not so much directed against the enemy;
rather the aim is to expand the networks of extremism' (ibid.:
121). Techniques of terror, 'ethnic cleansing' or genocide become
deliberate war strategies in the pursuit of specific political aims
and objectives. Outright battles are rare; instead, in these new
wars, violence is directed mainly against civilians. 'Violations
of humanitarian and human rights law are not a side effect of
war', she adds, 'but the central methodology of new wars' (ibid.).
That is to say, the visibility of human suffering in these wars, in
which news media play a central role, becomes a weapon itself in
the shared narrative of political extremism which holds many of
these networks together.

In this way, then, new wars are challenging prevailing perceptions of war itself. What were once distinct local, national
and global realms are now seen to be converging, while traditional divisions – not least between war and crime – effectively
blur into a particularistic, divisive identity politics. Throughout,
media channels are prominent in the organizing logics of the
conduct of war. The value of the wider frameworks provided by
Der Derian, Kaldor and others is readily apparent at a number
of different levels. Scholarly treatments of war reporting tend to
gloss over the nature of war itself, preferring to rely upon certain
teleological assumptions about how the evolution of war-fighting
strategies has unfolded over the years. On those occasions when

the familiar tenets of the 'old' wars of the twentieth century are challenged, more often than not they are regarded as exceptions to certain longstanding (Clausewitzean, in military parlance) beliefs in modern war as a rational instrument in the service of advancing state interests. And yet, it seems, the growing number of these exceptions – what Manuel Castells (2000) calls 'instant wars' – is inviting a radical reconsideration of the familiar assumptions associated with prevailing discourses of war.

This context figures heavily in our account of the endeavours of journalists to record contemporary conflict. The extraordinarily high casualty rate among journalists in Iraq during the peak years of the US invasion and occupation, for example, is attributable partly to the new freedom which portable communications equipment gave them to enter dangerous areas, but it is also related to the collapse of the notion of the journalist as neutral observer which the frameworks discussed above make readily apparent. The distinction between combatant and reporter increasingly makes little sense to those fighting modern war. Kevin Sites, to return to our opening example, emerges as a figure caught between a professional ethics, which requires that the correspondent remain an external observer to events, and the knowledge that reporting an ostensible war crime will be regarded by some military and political authorities as tantamount to supporting the enemy. The always constricted space for independent war reporting tightens still further in the context of new wars.

Pertinent in this regard is Tumber and Webster's (2006) examination of the journalistic practices of front-line correspondents, which has led them to elaborate a conception of 'information wars' to address the ways in which they see the geometry of communicative power being transformed. Efforts to understand the use of 'virtuoso technologies' to deliver 'astonishing pictures and sounds from the theatre of war' to audiences in distant places, they argue, must not overlook the wider information environment shaping the interpretation of unpredictable events and their significance:

> First of all, frontline journalists are not easily controlled or manipulated to act as conduits for combatants and their leaders. They have a strong disposition towards 'telling it like it is', they cling to notions of 'objectivity' and they have access to versatile equipment that allows them to report quickly and immediately back to their news organizations. Furthermore, the boundaries between fighting forces are often confused and, perhaps more important, journalists are such a diverse group that once-powerful appeals to support 'our boys' have weakened. Moreover, while embeds are severely constrained by virtue of their locations, news organizations now receive an enormous volume and variety of information. What gets into a finished programme or news report may be quite at odds with any single journalist's report. (Tumber and Webster, 2006: 172)

While military weaponry may reflect a massive asymmetry between combatants, it follows, there can be no corresponding assumption that it will engender long-term success in the waging of information war. In the age of the digital camera and the website, Tumber and Webster point out, weaker forces ('who are acutely conscious that the media are globalized phenomena') can disrupt, challenge and often counter the imposition of truth claims by the powerful.

We shall be returning to the questions raised by these varied conceptions of war – 'virtuous war', 'new war' (including 'network' and 'spectacle' warfare) and 'information war' – in the chapters to follow. In the next section, we pause to place journalism within digital culture more widely, another important dimension informing much of this book's discussion.

Journalism and digital culture

Researchers interested in examining the dynamics of mediation often point out that traditional conceptions of 'the audience' lack adequate explanatory power in the age of digital media. Any notion of 'the audience' as a homogenous group with passive responses to 'media effects' can be safely dispensed with, they contend, once attention turns to the socially contingent ways in which mediation is negotiated in everyday circumstances. In the case of social networking sites, blogs or home videos posted on file-sharing sites, for example, there is ample evidence that the familiar distinction between 'the media' and 'the masses' cannot be sustained. Jenkins (2006) identifies a shift which he terms 'convergence culture', in which 'old' and 'new' media are colliding in conflicts over ownership of popular culture and control over public debate. Deuze (2005) proposes that it is increasingly apparent that the twentieth-century conception of journalists as professional, public storytellers has been part of a passing historical moment. Citing enthusiasts of participatory media and cyberculture, he notes that media technologies such as cell phones, wireless internet and plug-and-play have made self-mediation by individuals both easier and more public, but also more acceptable in terms of wider Western culture. Deuze links these practices to Bauman's (2000) notion of the 'liquidness' of contemporary Western society, in which traditional, fixed identities and relationships such as those of work, marriage and belonging are more prone to change over an individual's life, and in which the project of self-construction rises to prominence. The professional journalist's hold over public storytelling becomes weaker in this context, he argues, as people regard themselves less as audiences for media and more as producers, and as they consider their own media production to be at least as legitimate. 'It then seems the astounding rise of the mass media throughout the twentieth century owes much of its success to filling a temporary void between the demise of our trust in (as well as reliance on and allegiance to) social institutions – like the state, the church or mosque, the school, our families or our parents – and the emergence of a perhaps over-zealous faith in ourselves' (Deuze, 2005; see also Hassan, 2008).

Other scholars express caution as to the extent of any actual cultural shift. Some note that economic power over media remains vested largely in large corporations such as News Corporation, which has broadened its media holdings into the likes of MySpace, and that little has changed with the advent of corporate control of the web other than some fresh packaging for existing products and 'efficiency gains' as those products are 'repurposed' for online users (see Scott, 2005). Others point out that much 'citizen media' echoes the cultural norms and values of products found in mainstream media to a large extent, and indeed is typically dependent upon established media for material, and indeed for the social status of its leading practitioners (see Haas, 2005). Relevant here is evidence pertinent to journalism's evolving relationship with its publics, raising searching questions about authority, trust and even legitimacy. At a time when news organizations find themselves under intense recessionary pressures, with large-scale job losses having detrimental effects on the quality of provision, the very viability of certain leading institutions is open to question. Some commentators envisage the emergence of a post-journalism age as a logical extension of a 'democratized' media, while others are content to describe the demise of specific genres of journalism, such as the newspaper, in nostalgic terms. There is nothing new about such predictions, of course. Some years ago researchers such as Bardoel (1996) were suggesting that journalists were no longer indispensable in public communication and therefore must demonstrate anew their value, evolving to meet the changing needs of publics. A steady stream of news executives, editors and journalists have similarly expressed their concern that audiences – especially younger people – now demand news in a less formal style and a more flexible format, that few put faith in the credibility of the masthead as a guarantor of reportorial integrity, and that journalists must descend from their remote, detached position in public life and begin to interact with their audiences much more directly.

The specific responses by news organizations – launching podcasts of programmes, investing in editors' blogs, inviting viewers to contribute video, and the like – are better analysed elsewhere (see, for example, Allan, 2006; Boczkowski, 2004; Friend and Singer, 2007; Kawamoto, 2003; Paterson and Domingo, 2008). What concerns us here is the wider context for these developments. Bruns (2008) proposes that a second tier of media of public debate has emerged – as envisioned by Gans (1980) nearly thirty years previously – which comments on, critiques and reinterprets the news media for different communities. Leadbetter and Miller (2004) trace a trend for people to invest time and energy in unpaid work to professional standard, which they argue signals a shift towards bottom-up self-organization and the decline of professional authority in society in general (see also Keen, 2007). On many levels, previously secure and distinct categories of the media producer and consumer have begun to blur. In light of these and similar arguments, there is value in addressing the proliferation of public or citizen digital media, from photo-sharing websites to blogs, precisely as they recast what counts as journalism – and thereby who can be a journalist (see also Allan and Thorsen, 2009; Matheson, 2009). Theories of digital media, while at times prone to sweeping generalizations, make a convincing case that attention should be paid to the epistemological commitments underpinning the very idea of journalism, a position with important implications – as we shall see – for war reporting.

Digital war reporting

Theoretical frameworks such as these provide the impetus for us to move beyond bold pronouncements – both celebratory and condemnatory alike – regarding digitalization and convergence in order to gain a critical purchase on the issues that matter most for socially responsible war reporting. They will emerge throughout the book and inform the choice of material and the arguments proposed here. In this section, we offer a brief overview of this volume's organizational rationale and the contents of its respective chapters.

First, though, it is worth signposting the large and growing literature on the relationship between journalism and war, where the importance of technology is often acknowledged. Conflicts involving the US and Britain in the post-Cold War era, in particular, have attracted a flurry of academic interest, especially in the past decade. In pausing to highlight briefly the impressive range of studies on offer, we recognize the value and diversity of perspectives on offer within journalism studies (in the case of the war in Iraq, for example, see Allan and Zelizer, 2004; Artz and Kamalipour, 2005; Bennett et al., 2007; Berenger, 2004; Debrix, 2007; El-Nawawy and Iskander, 2003; Hammond, 2007; Hoskins, 2004; Kavoori and Fraley, 2006; Kellner, 2005; Knightley, 2004; Lewis, 2006; Maltby and Keeble, 2007; Miller, 2004; Mirzoeff, 2005; Moeller, 2009; Norris et al., 2003; Nossek et al., 2007; Seaton, 2005; Seib, 2004; Sylvester and Huffman, 2005; Tumber and Palmer, 2004; Tumber and Webster, 2006; among others). Consistent across a large share of these enquiries is a concern with the perceived alignment of war reporting with the national interest in times of war – that is, the pressures brought to bear upon journalism to ensure that it helps to create and maintain patriotic support for the war effort. Some go further, questioning the extent to which journalism has become complicit in promoting officially sanctioned definitions of the very nature of war itself, such that voices of dissent are effectively marginalized or trivialized, if not silenced altogether. Journalism, such critiques contend, has been effectively transformed into a vital cog in the machinery of war.

It is against this backdrop that *Digital War Reporting* will make its own contribution, namely by focusing directly on the ways in which digital technologies are shaping what is reported, how and why. The time span which unfolds over the chapters to follow covers the better part of a decade, namely from what has been dubbed the 'first internet war' in Kosovo in 1999 to recent crises in South Ossetia and Mumbai, respectively. Given the rather formidable task of covering so much ground in a book of relatively modest length, we have been necessarily selective in our choice of topics and case studies. Accordingly, rather than seeking to be comprehensive in the scope of our discussion, we hope that it will contribute to the conceptual formalization of this area of enquiry. In resisting the pull of easy binaries – utopian/dystopian renderings of the promise/threat posed by digital technologies

– we shall concentrate our attention on exploring the emergence and consolidation of different modes of war reporting over the last decade. The identification of certain technical innovations is important, we shall argue, but equally significant are the ways in which these innovations were taken up and modified in routine, everyday practice. Such a focus on the uses of digital technology pinpoints the ways in which the capacity of the journalist to bear witness to the atrocities of wartime is contingent upon the lived negotiation of its possibilities, as well as on its pressures and constraints. In what ways, we shall ask, has the gradual consolidation of various technologies affected news content, the repertoire of sourcing strategies available, or the genres of presentation? Moreover, to what extent have successive innovations reaffirmed, challenged or transformed the war reporter's social responsibilities in times of national crisis?

With these questions in mind, our attention turns in the next chapter to 'the first internet war', as it was widely dubbed by journalists and press commentators with respect to the reporting of Kosovo in 1999. 'The battle for hearts and minds is being fought on the net', declared *The Guardian*'s reporter Simon Rogers at the time, an observation that underscored the rapidly growing significance of web-based journalism. Deserving of particular attention, other observers agreed, was the way these new forms of reporting afforded members of the public in distant places unprecedented degrees of access and immediacy to breaking news events in the war zone. This chapter seeks to explore a range of factors shaping this emergent ecology of digital war coverage, including the extent to which it invited a self-reflexive critique among journalists about the relative challenges these technologies posed for the integrity of reportorial practice. Those welcoming the arrival of digital technologies – the internet, but also satellite dishes, laptops, cell phones, audio and video recorders, and the like – encountered the reservations of critics, many of whom were sceptical about the relative advantages to be gained by 'cyber-journalism' where improving war reporting was concerned. In discerning the contours of this debate, this chapter considers a number of issues, not least the use of the internet as an alternative platform for the eyewitness accounts of ordinary citizens. In so doing, it offers an evaluative appraisal of processes often obscured by the rhetoric surrounding the perceived capacity of digital technologies to create a heightened personal engagement for 'us' with the distant suffering of 'them'.

Chapter 3 focuses on the enormous increase in the use of digital media to communicate war during the West's military involvement in Afghanistan (2001–) and Iraq (2003–). In particular, it emphasizes the desire within journalism to use these tools to produce accounts of contemporary conflict that can sustain a claim to be more 'real'. As journalists have become equipped with technologies which make them dramatically more mobile than in   ce to be
conden   s permit
differei   ted. On
the one   se wars,
the hig   llapsing
into th   , as live
reporti   orogress
of arm   e widely
critiqui   iestions
about t   halism's
indepe   ; well as
the thi   id speed
of new   ice rich,
diverse   ticularly
more i   became
widely   in ways
that opened up alternative realities of war. Experiments by news organizations and self-supporting reporters alike gave particular emphasis to subjective and experiential forms of reporting, in which the relationship between journalist and audience could be renegotiated and in which the journalist's location in the war zone was more prominent than his or her location within the news institution. In what can be seen as a reaction against the

limited views of conflict available in embedded and live reporting, these forms became identified with longstanding conceptions of the war correspondent as an independent individual with a moral commitment to bear witness to war, yet in the process rearticulated those traditions.

Chapter 4 takes these themes further. As experiential, subjective and interpersonal forms of communication became identified with a richer and potentially more comprehensive view of the reality of conflict, it became harder to sustain a distinction between reporting by journalists and self-mediation by others in the war zone, whether participants, observers or victims. In Iraq and then in the 2005 war in Lebanon and later conflicts, journalism's accounts of war and political violence have become contested as authoritative or authentic by this plethora of other voices. The chapter explores the complex relationship between these new media and journalism, from the assimilation of citizen journalism and witness accounts within the news to the enormous potential of media produced on the edges of dominant institutions to open up new public spaces to the increasing politicization and even 'weaponization' of the representation of war by combatants and their supporters. No simple claims, then, can be made for the power of interactive digital media to enhance democracy or hold to account those who commit violence in pursuit of political ends. To an extent, the chapter concludes, citizen media have become another space of war, whose potential to give communicative power back to ordinary soldiers or to citizens caught up in war is at constant risk of being subverted by attempts to mobilize that power as part of the conflict.

The visual culture of digital war reporting is centred for examination in chapter 5. For photographers confronted with the challenge of bearing witness to violence unfolding around them, the effort to record its human consequences is an acutely interpretive – and therefore political – process. Images can range from those shot by photojournalists striving to produce an impartial record, to ones taken for entirely different reasons by participants in the violence, or even those captured by ordinary citizens who happen to be in the wrong place at the wrong time, among other possibilities. Despite these differences, however, this imagery recurrently exhibits a shared commitment to 'making real' the horrors of events in war zones. Accordingly, this chapter aims to offer an evaluative assessment of this capacity, both in theoretical terms and with respect to its practical realization vis-à-vis specific examples. The discussion begins with an assessment of the debate that erupted when a professional photojournalist elected to digitally manipulate an image taken of soldiers and civilians in Iraq, a hastily made decision for largely aesthetic reasons that proved to have far-reaching implications for journalistic integrity. Next, our attention turns to the controversies sparked by photographs taken by amateurs, including those of US soldiers' coffins being transported home, of torture in Abu Ghraib prison, and of the execution of Saddam Hussein. It will be shown that 'our camera-mediated knowledge of war', to use Susan Sontag's (2003) evocative phrase, raises important questions about the mediation of communicative power in a digital age.

Finally, the discussion draws to a close in chapter 6. Here we pull together a number of threads of the book through an exploration of the politics of mediation discernible in various struggles over the digital reporting of recent conflicts. Set against the context of normative expectations of communication technologies as spaces of democratization, the chapter describes the various political uses of such media and their consequences. In devoting particular consideration to the form of emergent reporting practices, it highlights modes of communication promising to help narrow the 'culture of distance' (Williams, 1982) in ways that invite emphatic, moral engagement. In doing so it draws attention to the way in which the subjectivity of the reporter can itself be deployed in a claim to speak in universal human terms, and to the way in which individuals can use journalism as a resource to advance further collective endeavours symbolically to resist war. The chapter's underlying theme, and a central thread in the book's argument, is that the rhetoric of war legitimizes certain configurations of 'us and them' which must be identified and challenged. Digital war reporting has a vitally important role to play in this regard, we shall argue, not least where a commitment to interactivity (and with it a diversity of perspectives) can open up for scrutiny the preferred terms of official truth claims so as to help engender public dialogue and debate.

CHAPTER TWO

The 'First Internet War'

Introduction

'Television broadcasts delivered Vietnam, with all its bloody, muddy anguish and fatigue, direct to our living rooms', journalist Carol Guensburg (1999) has observed. 'CNN gave us rooftop views of Baghdad and Pentagon-sanctioned glimpses of the Persian Gulf War that liberated Kuwait. Now, the internet has emerged as a force in bringing the Kosovo crisis up close and personal.' Guensburg's comments, while rehearsing a familiar form of shorthand where descriptions of war reporting are concerned, succeed in highlighting how changes in reportorial perspective can be shaped by technology in important ways. Deserving of particular attention, other commentators agreed, was the way the internet afforded members of the public in distant places unprecedented degrees of access and immediacy to breaking news events in the war zone.

Whether or not 'the first internet war' – a phrase put into public circulation by newspaper critics in the main – was an appropriate way to characterize the role of the web in the reporting of the Kosovo conflict was a question of a different order, however. Participants in the ensuing debate, not least war reporters themselves, tended to divide into two polarized positions. For those who welcomed the arrival of digital technologies – the internet, but also satellite dishes, laptops, cell phones, audio and video recorders, and the like – the advantages to be gained by 'cyber-journalism' could be measured in relation to factors such as the provision of online spaces for alternative viewpoints, background materials, eyewitness accounts and interactivity with audiences. For critics, in sharp contrast, there was the perception that the 'hype' about technology was obscuring the guiding principles of rigorous – and responsible – war journalism, with potentially dangerous consequences. Lost in the cascade of digital imagery, they feared, was a compelling rendering of what was actually happening on the ground, an account that offered carefully crafted insight, explanation and context. 'Liveness' and 'immediacy', it seemed, were often being valued for their own sake, which risked inviting a certain sense of detachment despite the rhetoric surrounding the capacity of digital technologies to create a heightened personal engagement.

This chapter, in taking as its principal focus the reporting of the Kosovo conflict in 1999, seeks to explore a range of issues warranting close scrutiny. Building upon our earlier references to the Persian Gulf War, it will be shown how the emergent ecology of digital war reporting continued to evolve, as well as the extent to which it invited a self-reflexive critique among journalists about the relative challenges these technologies posed for the integrity of reportorial practice. Of the various factors recasting war coverage in Kosovo, none was more important than the internet as an alternative platform for reporting. Beyond the rhetoric of 'Web War I', rudimentary forms of online reporting attracted considerable attention – many of them revolving around eyewitness accounts, photographs, video and audio clips circulated via e-mails, message boards, online diaries (the word 'blog', let alone 'warblog', yet to receive mainstream recognition), and so forth. Taken together, these forms signalled the increasingly significant involvement of ostensibly independent 'amateurs' as personal reporters – predecessors, in some ways, of what would evolve into the citizen journalism movement in years to come. In exploring the emergent tenets of internet-based war reporting, this chapter offers an evaluative appraisal of its rudimentary features as they slowly began to consolidate into the conventions known to us today.

Waging infowar

In the aftermath of the Persian Gulf War of 1991, a recurrent theme in appraisals of how the conflict had been reported was the significance of military jargon ('surgical strikes', 'smart bombs', 'collateral damage', 'friendly fire', 'soft targets', 'acceptable losses', and so forth). War reporters were criticized by some commentators for their apparent willingness to reprocess the military's preferred terminology, and with it certain ideological presuppositions, which helped effectively to 'sanitize' the reality of the conflict for news audiences. Widely recognized was the extent to which officials had actively sought to frame the conflict in particular ways through a variety of different rhetorical strategies. At stake was a greater aim than sustaining public support for the waging of war – officials, it appeared in retrospect, were also intent on changing public perception of the very nature of modern warfare itself. The failures associated with the so-called Vietnam syndrome, one official after another claimed at the time, had finally been set aside, thanks to the victory in the Gulf. History was being rewritten, some critics argued, with the unintentional co-operation of war reporters. Cumings, in his book *War and television*, made the point succinctly:

> Remember the Gulf War? Or was that last season's hit show? The Gulf War was a war fought to demolish a memory, but it was also a war that produced no memory. It was our first 'television war': not blood and guts spilled in living color on the living room rug, not the transparent, objective immediacy of the all-seeing eye . . . but a radically distanced, technically controlled, eminently 'cool' postmodern optic which, in the doing, became an instrument of the war itself. (1992: 103)

Routinely displaced from this 'postmodern optic' was human death and suffering. The rapid diffusion of new techniques in war reporting – the 'real-time' reporting of CNN being the most widely celebrated – was transforming the conduct of war itself, or so it seemed. Extraordinary footage of laser-guided 'smart' bombs and 'clean' missiles 'removing targets' made for spectacular television visuals, some of it shot through 'full motion cockpit videos' from a safe distance above. 'There was none of the agony of the burned and wounded that had been glimpsed on television relays from Vietnam', Franklin argued. 'In this magnificent triumph of techno-war, America's images of its wars had reached perfection' (1994: 42).

Also during 1991, however, very different types of images were appearing on Western television screens as the violent break-up of the former Yugoslavia gathered momentum. 'No other conflict – not even the Gulf war, which took on the character of a made-for-television CNN special event – has been fought so much in public, under the eye of the camera', recalled the BBC's Martin Bell (1995: 137) about Bosnia. In the 'decade of the dish', as he characterized it, the 'satellite is as much a weapon of war as the sniper's rifle, and the soundbite is an extension of warfare by other means' (ibid.: 139). For all three parties to the war, the Serbs, Croats and Muslims, the idea of television as an independent service was ridiculous, he argued. Instead, it was made to operate as a medium of control as much as one of information for their respective peoples. For Western journalists, able to report without the pressures of political censorship, the most difficult challenges were engendered by more subtle forms of self-censorship, not least where the medium itself – namely 'its thirst for immediacy and its idolatry of the live shot' – was concerned. '[We] congratulate ourselves on our talent and technology, on how fast and wonderful we are, on how we can pitch our dishes wherever the news breaks, and how we can bring you the world in twenty-two minutes' (ibid.: 208), Bell maintained, and yet editorial guidelines about the depiction of on-screen violence proved to have a powerful influence on what was covered, and how. Apprehensions about how audiences might respond to broadcast images of 'the human price being paid' led to what Bell terms 'good taste' censorship. Consequently, he adds, 'in our anxiety not to offend and upset people, we were not only sanitizing war but even *prettifying* it, as if it were an acceptable way of settling disputes, and its victims never bled to death but rather expired gracefully out of sight.' This when 'war is real and war is terrible', he added. 'War is a bad taste business' (ibid.: 216).

Debates about the capacity of 'real-time' television news to sanitize the horrors of warfare resurfaced in press commentary over the next few years on a regular basis, but most prominently following the commencement of NATO's bombing campaign in Kosovo. Images eerily reminiscent of the 'techno-war' waged in Iraq appeared on Western television screens on 24 March 1999, as war reporters struggled to perform 'rooftop journalism' from the vantage point of their hotels in Belgrade. CNN was particularly successful in secretly capturing footage of the NATO air raids, showing viewers green fluorescent 'nightscope' images of the strikes. The Serb authorities moved quickly, taking twenty-nine of the reporters into custody. In the case of CNN's Brent Sadler and his crew, for example, they were shocked to hear their hotel room door being broken down by an armed man later that night. 'I thought it was curtains', Sadler later recalled. 'They felt we were part of the whole attack structure' (cited in Ricchiardi, 1999). Instead, the intruders were intent on damaging the crew's equipment and rummaging through their notes and files. The next morning, having been ordered to leave the country, members of the crew were physically accosted before watching their remaining equipment smashed again, and an armoured car set alight. According to a *New York Times* report, crowds of Serbian passers-by cheered at the sight, while frightened fellow journalists watched from the relative safety of the hotel's lobby (26 March 1999). This was to be expected, suggested Justin Raimondo (1999) in an entry in his 'Wartime diary' posted on Antiwar.com that day. '[T]hose Western journalists who have placed themselves and their profession in the service of [the] Allied Force should not be too surprised to find that the people they have demonized are less than hospitable', he maintained. Presumably the feeling was mutual for the journalists involved, given that Serbian propaganda had attempted to 'demonize' them (such was the view of CNN's Eason Jordan, who complained that the network was routinely singled out for being a 'factory of lies' – indeed, shortly thereafter, he rendered the claim that 'Serbia has essentially declared war on CNN'; see Littlefield, 1999).

Within two days, most of the journalists from NATO countries had been summarily transported to the border. The expulsion order, issued by the Serbian information minister, Aleksandar Vučić, was succinct: 'Journalists of foreign public media from the countries that took part or allowed their territories to be used in NATO aggression on our country will be expelled.' Those allowed to remain faced severe restrictions on what they could report. Some proved remarkably resourceful in getting the story out by using what freelancer Kevin McAuliffe (1999) termed 'advances in the Information Revolution – satellite dishes more mobile than ever, cell phones more reliable ("half of the good interviews I've gotten I got while driving," says [*Time* magazine's Massimo] Calabresi), satellite phones with longer battery life'. In McAuliffe's view, the 'SATphones, though still bulky, proved to be the big breakthrough weapon for the media in the early stages of the conflict – enabling reporters equipped with laptop, modem, and disk to transmit entire stories from wherever they were.' Nevertheless, as McAuliffe was quick to acknowledge, 'no amount of technology can take the place of solid on-the-spot reporting', which meant that efforts to tell a more complete story were being frustrated by the lack of access. Indeed, as Ricchiardi (1999) pointed out, once the NATO bombing campaign was under way, 'news executives [in the US] lost sleep over the safety of their forces in the field and turned to cyberspace – e-mail and the internet – in attempts to move the story forward.' At the same time, she added, they 'also began the agonizing process of determining how to get correspondents back into a country that had declared itself a journalist-free zone.'

Meanwhile, an unexpected dimension to the conflict was unfolding. Press commentators were increasingly drawing attention to what was being dubbed 'cyberwar', by which they meant the heated battle over ideas being fought across the internet. Governments on both sides had mobilized resources to communicate – or, more typically, to propagandize – their point of view. The US State Department and the White House, like the Foreign and Commonwealth Office and Downing Street in the UK, ensured that their websites provided constant updates. In addition, some carried official speeches and transcripts of press briefings – as well as charts, maps, photographs, and audio and video facilities – to serve as 'background information' about the conflict for users to download. The Yugoslavian state, in seeking to counter what it perceived to be Western propaganda, was equally committed to advancing its interests via its web presence. For example, acts of what it described as Kosovo Albanian terrorism – including those said to be perpetrated by 'KLA [Kosovo Liberation Army] guerrillas' – were evidence, in its view, of genocide committed against Serbs under the cover of NATO cruise missiles. Similarly, the posting of news stories such as 'Criminal NATO Air Force hits only civilians' (2 April 1999) made clear the preferred perspective. At the same time, the e-mail addresses of Western news organizations were circulated via bulletin boards with a view to encouraging the sending of criticism and complaints. Mark Schreiner cites one example sent to his newspaper:

> Hungarians, Bulgarians, Gypsies, Croats, Romanians who are under attack from NATO and who are sending you these e-mails to you to let you know what is being done in your name . . . They would like you to know that your 'democratic media,' which is using its reports from the war in Yugoslavia to sell more consumer goods . . . is lying about the NATO targets as well. (Schreiner, 1999)

Information was virtually indistinguishable from propaganda in this climate of suspicion, making trustworthy facts increasingly difficult to ascertain. 'It used to be that warriors on both sides of a conflict – grunts and generals, politicians and diplomats – made their cases through the war correspondent, who sifted the facts from the spin', observed Don North (1999). 'Now combatants often try to bypass the press, communicating their information and viewpoints directly to the world via the Internet.'

Images of so-called precision bombing were part of NATO's information strategy during its attacks on Serbian-controlled Kosovo, in stark contrast to the personal and often powerfully emotional responses of civilians in web-based media (May 1999). © Corbis

NATO's 'information warfare' strategy, which included a psychological operations (PSYOPS) campaign, was being countered at each turn by the Yugoslav government's efforts to withstand it. 'Now the Web is a vivid mirror of the struggle for Kosovo, a first in war', *Newsweek* magazine (12 April 1999) maintained. It proceeded to identify brief examples of how the conflict was being reported online – specifically, with regard to access ('The Hague tribunal revealed the indictment of Serb militia leader "Arkan" [an alleged war criminal] – and he chatted live on msnbc. com'), intelligence ('NATO announced Web sites for the reporting of war crimes by witnesses in Kosovo'), mischief ('Belgrade hackers temporarily disabled NATO's main Web site by bombarding it with empty messages') and propaganda ('Pro-Serb sites denounced NATO "insanity" and "terrorism" by Kosovars. One extreme page: www.kosovo.net'). Such 'mischief' took a variety of forms. NATO's website, described in some press accounts as 'the first cyber casualty', struggled to remain operational in the face of e-mails with gigabyte files attached, spam, and 'ping' or 'denial of service' attacks ostensibly launched by hackers in Serbia. These forms of 'cyber-terrorism' were surprisingly successful both in 'defacing' and crashing this site, as well as a range of others in the US (including that of the Department of Defense and whitehouse.gov – the latter evidently unable to send documents for a week). Shortly after they were restored, however, they faced a further onslaught of 'cyber-attacks', this time allegedly from Chinese hackers enraged by the NATO attack on the Chinese embassy in Belgrade on 8 May 1999, which left three journalists dead and twenty diplomats injured. NATO's claims that the bombing was accidental were dismissed and a range of government sites were hacked. The US Department of Energy's home page, for example, was rewritten to state:

> Protest USA's Nazi action! Protest NATO's brutal action! We are Chinese hackers who take no cares about politics. But we can not stand by seeing our Chinese reporters been killed which you might have know. Whatever the purpose is, NATO led by USA must take absolute responsibility. You have owed Chinese people a bloody debt which you must pay for. We won't stop attacking until the war stops!

In China itself, hackers reportedly defaced the website for the US embassy in Beijing, posting the phrase 'Down with the barbarians' in Chinese on its homepage.

The fierce controversy regarding whether or not NATO's missile strike on the Chinese embassy was accidental – a 'diplomatic calamity' in the words of *The Observer* newspaper – would continue for some time. Critics maintained it was part of a wider strategy to control the flow of information at all costs, pointing to a range of NATO attacks launched against the civilian communications infrastructure (including the targeting of the head office of Radio Television Serbia, killing sixteen journalists and other employees, a fortnight earlier). Information warfare, it was becoming increasingly clear, did not respect familiar boundaries. Vital to recognize in this regard, as Goodman pointed out, was

the extent to which the status of news organizations was being
defined in these terms. 'The speed of communications, like
the speed of a missile, affects and influences the substance of
the message and its propaganda value just as the accuracy of the
modern missile can select (if not always hit) an oil installation or
a television station at the touch of a computer button', he wrote
in the *British Journalism Review*. 'The media, and therefore working journalists, have now become prime targets – for destruction
as well as for influencing' (G. Goodman, 1999: 5). More routine, however, were the strategies employed by military officials
severely to restrict information flow on a day-to-day basis. 'And
what information was released', Kitfield (1999) pointed out in
the *National Journal*, 'was managed, massaged, and manipulated
by NATO and the Pentagon – as NATO spokesman Jamie Shea
later acknowledged – with an eye to filling up airtime with the
alliance's message of the day, rather than filling in the blanks for
the thirsty media and the uninformed public.' To the extent that
'official' news occupied the 'media space', it followed, journalists
would be supplied with sufficient amounts of 'fresh information to report on' so as to diminish the likelihood that they would
pursue 'critical stories' on their own (see also Kitfield, 2001).

Evidently, then, any notion of Kosovo as a 'techno-war' revolved
around the battle to control information. Nicholas Barber (1999),
writing in *The Scotsman* at the height of the conflict, affirmed this
point. 'The central tension of reporting the current war is that
between openness and restriction', he observed, 'between the
gush of information that digital technology and a rolling news
format can provide and the clamping down on that information
by the relevant governments.' This tension, first acknowledged
as a significant difficulty to be negotiated in the reporting of the
Gulf War, was being exacerbated ever more deeply in Kosovo.
'Foreign policy becomes the victim of what we call the CNN
effect', veteran journalist Daniel Schorr stated. 'In the age of
television, what we face is that everything is told the way television sees it.' The 24-hour cycle of image-led reporting impacts,
in turn, on the very events under scrutiny. 'Television cannot see

ideas, television cannot see philosophy – but it can see things happening, especially violent things', Schorr contended. 'What results is that our foreign philosophy is now driven by what people see on television' (cited in Littlefield, 1999). This argument was proving to be as valid in Kosovo as it had been in the Gulf, with the major difference being that the authority of television news was being compromised by difficulties in securing access. Unable to bear witness to the actual fighting, journalists were relying on interview material gathered from the exodus of refugees fleeing the attacks. 'The biggest story we have is of the refugees leaving', commented Bill Wardman, Sky foreign news editor, 'but the war itself is closed to us' (cited in Barber, 1999). Under such circumstances, journalists could do little more than report what the refugees were claiming, comparing and contrasting their accounts with official statements. Independent verification of what was happening on the ground remained frustratingly elusive.

Elsewhere, however, alternative forms of war reporting were emerging which, taken together, threw into sharp relief the constraints shaping mainstream news organizations' coverage. 'Underground', 'populist' or 'amateur' journalism, as it was variously labelled, performed by ordinary citizens using the web, was being increasingly recognized as a vitally important source of news. This type of war reporting, to the surprise – and chagrin – of some veteran correspondents, would have a profound impact on perceptions of the conflict.

Uncomfortable truths

'Last night two NATO airplanes came down not far from us. I spoke to my friends and they said: "let's go hunt pilots".' These words were attributed by The Guardian reporter Simon Rogers (1999) to an e-mail sent to the newspaper by a computer engineer in Belgrade. In his view, they constituted not only further evidence that the war in Kosovo 'could be the first fought on the Internet', but also that such e-mails could be regarded as a form of reporting in their own right. For Rogers, 'with western journalists thrown out of Yugoslavia, they are perhaps the last reliable source of information coming out of the war zone.'

A 'battle for hearts and minds', reporters such as Rogers were pointing out, was being fought in cyberspace. This point had been effectively underscored time and time again over the years by the steadfast efforts of Belgrade's only independent radio station, B92. A constant thorn in the side of the Milošević government since it first went on the air in May 1989, B92 had come to rely on the internet to maintain its operation. In December 1996, for example, that station's coverage of the anti-government demonstrations – which erupted following Serbian president Slobodan Milošević's annulment of municipal local elections won by the opposition – had led to its being banned from the airwaves. Managers had promptly prioritized its website, relying on digital broadcasts using RealAudio in English and Serbo-Croatian to continue its updates regarding growing protests on the streets. 'In the early days of the protests, before the international media arrived, it was the only way most people outside Belgrade could hear about what was happening', stated Sasa Vucinic, managing director of the non-profit Media Development Loan Fund. 'And the moment the radio signal from B92 was cut, the Internet took over. Mailboxes of government officials in Europe, humanitarian agencies, journalists and supporters were flooded within hours with the news of the closure' (cited in Hedges, 1996). Any success the Yugoslav authorities enjoyed with regard to the closing of transmitters could not be extended to the internet. 'We have mirror sites now in Europe and North America, and if they shut down the Belgrade server we can directly modem the information overseas', stated one student activist. 'To stop that they will need to shut down every telephone in Serbia – which is impossible' (cited in Bennahum, 1997). When the Milošević regime relented and allowed B92 to recommence broadcasting on the airwaves two days later, there was little doubt the station had won an important – if temporary – symbolic victory.

With its growing prominence in the world's press, B92

represented one of the more pronounced examples of how the internet was becoming a lifeline for oppositional groups, many of whom heralded the victory as evidence of 'the Internet Revolution' under way. Having been forced to rely on the web in order to circumvent government control, these groups were discovering to their surprise that the size of their audiences – both within the region and, crucially, well beyond it – could be dramatically increased. This point was proven again when the US-led NATO bombing campaign began in Kosovo in March 1999. Knocked off the air in the first hours of the attacks, B92 found its voice again via the internet. 'It's essential', Julia Glyn-Pickett, UK spokesperson for the station, maintained at the time. 'The people who have links print the information out and distribute it. People in Serbia are very aware of the sources of news and are very news hungry' (cited in Rogers, 1999). The crucial role of the internet in this regard was reaffirmed days later by Veran Matic (1999), chief editor, shortly after the police arrived to seal the station's doors. In his words:

> Our programme is still kept alive thanks to the Internet and a satellite link. For how long, nobody knows. B92's news services, available on our website in Serbian and English, are getting more than a million hits a day from people downloading our information, sending in messages of support and protesting against the Nato air strikes. We receive messages from all around the world, not only from the Serbs and Americans, but from virtually every spot on the globe. They are concerned and they worry about our safety. (Matic, 1999)

Arrested and detained for several hours, Matic could not stop the transmitter being confiscated, but www.b92.net carried on regardless (although regularly overwhelmed with the amount of traffic coming its way, slowing the load-time of URLs to several minutes). Operating clandestinely from secret locations, the station was relying, once again, on a consortium of international media organizations based in Amsterdam to relay its provision via mirror sites. 'The information available is extremely limited', one member of the B92 staff told a US journalist. 'In state of war – censorship rules apply. Serbian TV is showing "patriotic" reports and lifting up the spirit. We, B92, are virtually among the last bastions of balanced journalism' (cited in *USA Today*, 30 March 1999).

Few continued to dispute the status of the Kosovo crisis as the 'first internet war' by the time the bombing was under way. Of particular significance, however, was the contribution made by ordinary citizens posting their reports from near the very places where military weaponry was detonating with devastating effect. Appraisals of this new type of reportage frequently highlighted points of comparison with the first 'live' televised war in the Gulf in 1991. 'While the Persian Gulf War played like a made-for-TV event, with aerial shots of bombings and journalists sifting through rubble at the urging of Iraqi officials, the rules are dramatically different in the Balkans', argued newspaper journalist Jon Swartz (1999). 'Press restrictions in Yugoslavia have spawned a broad quilt of enterprising individuals and grass-roots organizations who are covering the conflict.' The internet has been 'a crucial tool', Fred Abrahams of Human Rights Watch concurred. 'Local journalists and human-rights activists are sending out every bit of news they can' (cited in Kanaley, 1999). Similarly involved in this capacity were individuals work-ing for refugee organizations as well as members of rescue operations. 'It's tailor-made for disaster relief work', stated Doug Rekenthaler, managing editor for DisasterRelief.org, about the internet. 'We can get to a disaster zone very quickly, write up some compelling copy about families victimized by the war, get in some digitized pictures.' A further advantage of such groups adopting a journalistic role for themselves, he added, was the constituency of readers that their efforts attracted on the web: 'the reader, wanting to help, can act: just point and click' (cited in Guensburg, 1999). Evidently it was the perceived virtue of this type of personal reportage – in contrast with the second-hand, highly mediated nature of mainstream news items – that helped to explain its popularity with web users.

Similarly garnering attention in this regard, in the press and on the web alike, were the efforts of self-fashioned war correspondents directly caught up in the conflict. So-called net dispatches, for example, were appearing in the mainstream news items with growing frequency, including those of Kosovo's 'cyber-monk' (as he was dubbed by the internet site Salon). Situated in a twelfthcentury monastery, Father Hieromonk Sava, a Serbian Orthodox monk, offered first-hand accounts based on news from 'the ground' gathered via an extensive range of internet and telephone contacts, as well as from Serbian refugees seeking shelter at the monastery. In sharp contrast to NATO pronouncements about the accuracy of strikes launched against military targets, he cited his range of 'credible sources' providing details about civilian facilities being destroyed as well. One such dispatch, filed from Decani, began: 'Despite the official promises by the Western governments that the attacks will be launched against military targets only, several civilian areas have already been hit' (cited in Kahney, 1999). This commitment to describing the human consequences of the bombing campaign informed Father Sava's reportage with a strong sense of purpose. 'It is my moral obligation', he wrote, 'to say that the statements by the NATO officials that only military targets are attacked in Yugoslavia are not true and they are intended to deceive many peace loving people in the West that their air force is in a "humanitarian" action' (Sava, 1999). In addition to his e-mail distribution list, Father Sava engaged in real-time chat using the monastery's website to distribute news reports, as well as his personal opinions about the crisis. The website, otherwise devoted to promoting peace and reconciliation, was effectively transformed into a site for independent reporting, attracting attention around the globe. Its independence was evidenced, in the main, by the heartfelt criticisms directed at both Slobodan Milošević's government and NATO. In the case of the latter, he wrote: 'We make a strong protest against these barbarous attacks which will make the humanitarian catastrophe much worse, in which the civilian population will suffer the most' (cited in North, 1999).

A further example of citizen-centred reportage attracting press attention revolved around a young teenager's efforts to communicate with her 'electronic pen pal' in the US. 'Adona', as she was known by her American high school friend, Finnegan Hamill, provided a glimpse into daily life in Kosovo through a number of e-mail messages. When sixteen-year-old Hamill, a reporter for Youth Radio in Berkeley, began broadcasting reports about her e-mails (with her permission) on National Public Radio's 'Morning Edition', national news media attention promptly followed. Dan Rather, then anchor of CBS News, introduced a story on the evening newscast as follows:

> Too often, when viewed from afar, war seems impersonal, so we have a different perspective tonight for you on the war inside Kosovo, a war between the mostly Orthodox Christian Serbs and the Muslims of Albanian heritage, who are in the majority. What you're about to hear in this report from CBS' John Blackstone, is the story of a teen-age girl caught in the war – a story told to her electronic pen pal here in the United States. (CBS News Transcripts, 25 March 1999)

The item continues, broadcasting excerpts of the e-mail correspondence read aloud:

> These are very critical moments here . . . The village is still surrounded. I can just hear planes passing . . . I really don't want to end up raped with no parts of body, like the massacred ones. I wish nobody in the world – in the whole universe would have to go through what we are . . . My brain, my whole life is just affected by reality. In just one picture of a dead, head-cut body, or a three-year-old child massacred, you would be affected, too. If you were the ones to taste this bitter and cruel part of the world, you would also understand the luckiness I feel for just being alive. Adona, Kosovo. (Ibid.)

The theme of 'impersonal' war reporting, signalled by Rather at the outset, guides the story's narrative throughout. Blackstone, the reporter responsible for the item, establishes from Hamill that Adona (her real name concealed for protection) is a sixteen-year-old Albanian Muslim. Her words are said to have made Hamill 'feel the suffering in all those images of a country torn by war'. This point is similarly taken up by Elizabeth Howton, writing in the *San Jose Mercury News*, who credits the student's radio reports – where Adona's words are read aloud by female students – with putting 'a human face on the war for millions of people around the country'. She quotes Hamill explaining his desire to establish a sense of connection, a point which assumes added poignancy when it is observed that Adona has not e-mailed since the start of the NATO bombing campaign the day before. 'Before, I would read the paper and see stories of war and think, that doesn't affect me', he stated. 'Since I've been writing with her, in every story I can see that there's somebody like Adona there being affected by this, a real person' (cited in Howton, 1999).

This sense of connection fostered by personal accounts on the internet highlighted an important way in which the familiar conventions of war reporting were being transformed. 'Night after night the network news offered a narrow prism of views, along with those ubiquitous aerial photos of NATO's bombing campaign', Lasica (1999) observed. 'The Internet, conversely, provided an alternative channel that offered deeper coverage, more interactivity and, most significantly, greater diversity of voices and viewpoints.' Examples of what this meant in practice abounded. Nenad Ćosić, a graphic designer living in Belgrade's city centre, established a webpage devoted to sharing breaking news of NATO's air strikes e-mailed to him from across the region. By midnight, e-mails are arriving every few seconds:

> 00:35 – 'In Zemun, we can hear planes and several detonations from the direction of Belgrade.'
> 00:36 – 'Loud detonations and planes flying over. Our air defense is fighting back. Good luck Belgrade.'
> 00:36 – 'Many explosions in Pancevo.'
> . . .
> 02:06 – 'About 10 bombs were dropped. I didn't count them well. I was confused and was lying on the floor. The whole sky above the airport is red.' (Cited in Jahn, 1999)

Evidently Ćosić devoted some eighteen hours a day to compiling accounts. Judging from claims made about the number of visitors to the website, the value of the 'early-alert system' was widely recognized. 'This has turned into a passion', he told an AP journalist. 'It gives me a feeling of doing something useful during this war' (ibid.). Not surprisingly, news organizations were quick to perceive the value of incorporating examples of e-mails or message-board statements into their news accounts, many of which afforded deeply emotive insights into the tragedy as it impacted upon ordinary lives. Examples included:

> Messiles [sic] started to fall like rains on Prishtina. Some five of them were seen and they were furtive. They looked like flames and falling like stars. One of them some perhaps one hour later, before the start of the NATO air strike, was so furtive that those watching from the windows felt the rush of the windblow on their nose and chest. Some few moments later, a big smoke and fire was observed on the Western side of Prishtina. (Cited in *Wired*, 26 March 1999)

> There are many executions going on . . . I didn't manage to make my family flee, so I am very concerned about their safety [sic]. You remember the Doctor [name withheld], he was executed last night. All, old part of Gjakova burned down. Several families are executed. Same was done in Prishtina, Vushtri, etc. Bajram Kelmendi with his two sons is executed. Sent [sic] this information wherever you can. (Cited in *Washington Post*, 29 March 1999)

> In Podujeva the situation is bad. We spoke to Uncle I last night and he said that the area of the city towards the brick factory was on fire. The Serbs burned down the house of R.S. He lived near the factory. Uncle I said that there are armed Serb paramilitary groups all over the city. He said that he has no idea where his family is. I hope this ends quick, and at the end . . . the people of Kosovo get to see some freedom. After all, I'd rather die from Nato bombs than from Serbian tortures, rapes, massacres. (Cited in *The Times*, 31 March 1999)

These types of statements, extraordinarily powerful in their emotional resonance, called into question not only what counted as 'news' from the region, but also who might be rightly labelled a journalist. 'Now the conflict in Kosovo is a chat room war, an e-mail war, a Web site war, a war in which anyone with a PC and a phone line can quite literally become a correspondent', stated Ellen Goodman (1999) in the *Boston Globe*, 'a war in which anyone with a netserver can log on to the war zone.'

This ad hoc 'DIY world of the net' emerging among ordinary people committed to sharing their personal accounts, views and interpretations of what was transpiring made effective use of the available technologies – including fax machines, e-mail, chat rooms and bulletin boards – to remarkable advantage. 'Limited as they are', Jennifer Frey (1999) observed in the *Washington Post*, 'these communications provide another glimpse inside Kosovo at a time when firsthand information is scarce.' She proceeded to note that, with so many Western journalists expelled from Kosovo, television pictures had become increasingly limited to those provided by Serbian state television. As a result, she added, 'the rest of the world is dependent on information gleaned from refugees streaming into nearby countries, and on other means – such as e-mail and phone calls – to understand the current situation in Kosovo.' In the case of the latter, internet chat rooms and message boards were providing spaces for first-person e-mailed accounts to circulate, but were also facilitating new forms of interpretation and critique. Pentagon silence about the downing of a stealth fighter, for example, was countered by message-board discussions about the wing markings shown on a Serbian television news item about the incident (where web users soon established that the markings were indeed those of an F-117a fighter previously based at Holloman air force base in New Mexico). The value of this type of analysis was recognized by web users around the world. 'The online pages have been much more valuable than TV and the papers', one US resident told his city's newspaper. 'I can go on bulletin boards and learn what is happening at that very moment' (*San Francisco Chronicle*, 27 March 1999). This point was echoed in the words of a computer engineer in Pittsburgh, who told the *New York Times*: 'The feeling is that we are participating in this war in a strange way because of the Internet. You feel like you have access to the information firsthand' (*New York Times*, 29 March 1999).

This type of war correspondence, with its human-to-human quality making a virtue of its inherent subjectivity, invited a range of journalistic views. 'Their first-hand accounts have the grainy texture of a war report, but without the distancing emotion that is more familiar in war correspondents', observed Charles Arthur in *The Independent* (13 April 1999). Similarly positive about the journalistic advantages to be gained were news organizations welcoming insights into how their coverage was being interpreted. 'We've had an ongoing conversation with about three dozen Serbs', stated Michael Moran, the international editor of the MSNBC.com site. 'They have questions about what we're doing, the motivation behind our coverage. And it's not been angry nonsense. They actually made some really good points.' For Moran it was nothing short of a 'revelation' to realize the way in which the web was creating a new basis for dialogue (cited in Regan, 1999). Adopting a more sceptical stance, however, were those who emphasized the need to ensure that material e-mailed (or found on the web) from unconfirmed sources was authentic. E-mail or board postings shared anonymously – including by senders anxious to protect their identities for fear of being arrested – posed particular problems for journalists seeking to ascertain the relative trustworthiness of claims. The challenge of verification was formidable, with the oft-rendered charge of 'propaganda masquerading as news' being at the forefront of news organizations' concerns. 'I think that's part of a new form of journalism', Ken Wolff, executive producer of CBC News Online, stated. The rules of verification were still being written where e-mail is concerned. 'My gut reaction is that most of them are [sincere] because there's some raw emotion that you can't fake', he believed. 'But we do have a policy to warn readers that e-mails must be taken for what they are' (cited in Flynn, 1999). These and related observations underscored the perceived news value of such content, as well as the growing recognition of the changing status of the internet as a news source in its own right.

Notwithstanding the reservations expressed by some, the internet's potential for 'communication across the battle lines' was registering in dramatic increases in the number of 'hits' experienced by news websites. CNN.com reported that interest in NATO's bombing campaign had led to some of the most intensive traffic in its history to date, from both near and far. Website statistics suggested that Yugoslavian usage increased by approximately 963 per cent by the end of March 1999, while users from around the world propelled the country from thirtieth place among foreign countries to sixth place on the CNN site's tally. Here the contrast with Iraq was telling. 'How the Internet's playing differently in this story, as opposed to Iraq, is that Yugoslavia is a wired country', Kerrin Roberts, CNN Interactive spokesperson, explained. 'It wasn't that our coverage was different. But the reaction is different. In this conflict, people are able to communicate directly in chat rooms with people in the conflict zone ... Here, it is a global community' (cited in Guensburg, 1999). Meanwhile something akin to 'an internet boom' was transpiring – albeit unevenly – across Yugoslavia itself, although the numbers of available internet connections remained tiny (most estimates suggesting that about 1 per cent of the population were able to go online). Access followed class lines, with the majority of users tending to be urban and relatively well educated – and, it was suggested in press accounts, less likely to be supportive of the authoritarian government. For those at the other end of the internet connection struggling to cope in a war zone, however, this capacity to communicate with distant others was truly invaluable. 'With the Internet we have the means of telling the world about how we feel about all this', Deana Srajber, a 29-year-old web designer, told one US newspaper. 'The frustrating part is that the world seems not to care how we feel' (*New York Times*, 29 March 1999).

The fog of digital war

'When war becomes a spectator sport, the media becomes the decisive theatre of operations', argued journalist and commentator Michael Ignatieff in his book *Virtual war* (1999). In the course of examining the nature of warfare as it emerged in the Balkans, he identified a range of issues which render problematic more traditional assumptions about 'real' wars in relation to 'virtual' ones. Singled out for particular attention in a virtual war, for example, is the way in which the presence of journalists in the field of operations constrains military actions while, at the same time, serving to redirect the focus of hostilities towards civilian opinion at home.

In the case of Kosovo, while the US-led NATO forces enjoyed overwhelming military superiority over the country's outdated air-defence system, Ignatieff contends that they were nonetheless surprisingly vulnerable to the changing dictates of public opinion back in the US. As a result, he points out, the Milošević government responded by engaging in an asymmetrical response of a different order: namely, it sought to use Western news reports documenting the horrors of war in a way that would undermine popular support for its continuation. This decision to 'exploit grisly incidents', he argued, proved to be remarkably effective:

> Western television crews duly reported the bombing of the Serbian television station, the Serbian socialist party headquarters, the train on the bridge, the refugee convoys in Kosovo. More than any other factor, this reportage sowed doubt in the minds of a Western electorate that had been in favor of military action when the bombing began. By the end of the operation, poll support for further bombing slipped below 50 percent for the first time, and it is doubtful that military action could have been continued much longer than it was. (Ignatieff, 1999: 193)

This dimension of war, Ignatieff insisted, was historically new, even though the conduct of modern warfare had been becoming increasingly transparent over recent decades (just as the relative distance between home and the battlefield was similarly diminishing). In his view, this meant that civilians were seeing war in a different way. It also meant, crucially, that journalists themselves were being transformed from observers into protagonists. 'In virtual war', he writes, 'journalists are turned, willingly or otherwise, into combatants' (ibid.). In this regard, he adds, they have little choice. Refusal to participate on Serb-organized tours of NATO attack sites would have meant being threatened with deportation ('or, what was worse, losing the pictures to their competitors'), yet to be involved was to risk the accusation of being a dupe of the Serbian government. Caught between both sides of the conflict, journalists struggled to mediate the deceptions intrinsic to war being fought on – and for – television. 'Virtual war is won', Ignatieff concludes, 'by being spun' (ibid.: 196).

Explanations for apparent shifts in public opinion about the legitimacy of the NATO intervention continue to be hotly contested, but an important factor at the time concerned the extent to which television viewers were surprised, even shocked, by images of what 'collateral damage' looked like. That is to say, for those who had found comfort in military discourses about clean air strikes launched with surgical precision, news reports bearing witness to the ensuing human carnage were likely to be deeply upsetting. Precision weaponry, such reporting demonstrated, could be tragically imprecise, with the consequences of 'mistakes' devastating. It was in this context, then, that the value of new digitized forms of war reporting – especially those made possible via the internet – needs to be situated. 'Instead of turning to the 6:30 news or having to wait for the morning New York Times to get comprehensive coverage of an international conflict, people are now turning to the Internet for the latest developments', stated Merrill Brown, editor in chief of MSNBC's online division. 'We had people on the scene filing stories, video and photos that captured the horror and scale of what was happening in utterly real time' (cited in Lasica, 1999).

Significant here was the growing perception that new forms of reporting in Kosovo were signalling that journalism, as Caldwell (1999) pointed out, was 'on the verge of a technology-driven revolution'. News organizations intent on making the most of the internet, he argued, had begun to use it as an 'information-collecting – not just information-disseminating – medium'. The implications of this apparent shift were difficult to discern at the time, but among advocates the emergence of what was promptly called 'new news' – that is, journalism of the web (rather than simply broadcast or newspaper coverage being placed online) – was overdue. For several major news organizations in the UK and the US, their web provision was now much more likely to be regarded as an increasingly important supplement to the main provision. 'We're not just a derivative of what's on the air', stated Katherine Dillon, manager of ABCNews.com, with respect to the network's nightly television newscast (cited in Crawley, 1999). It was a point of pride for journalists committed to the web provision to demonstrate its capacity to post material from the battlegrounds that was otherwise not available in the mainstream coverage. Television news reporters, Michael Moran of MSNBC. com pointed out, 'only get a minute and a half to tell their story on the nightly news, but the stuff that doesn't make it on to the evening news is the guts of a great Internet story' (cited in Regan, 1999). Internet-based reporting from a war zone remained a relatively rare occurrence, however. Kirk Spitzer, an assistant news editor for USAToday.com, was one of the very few internet-dedicated reporters to be dispatched to Yugoslavia. 'Through our live, on-site coverage, Spitzer was able to break an exclusive story on USAToday.com regarding the 14,000 Albanians forced from Macedonia refugee camps by government officials and left to defend for themselves', stated Jim Schulte, the website's editor-in-chief. 'He also has been filing journal entries that appear daily on USAToday.com, commenting on the Kosovo crisis from a personal perspective' (cited in PR Newswire, 19 April 1999).

This type of daily diary reporting – indicative of what would evolve into warblogging in the years to come – represented simply one of the many vital contributions made by the internet, at least in the eyes of its advocates. 'Too often, in today's sanitized press briefings, we forget that this is not about military targets and "collateral damage"', Lasica (1999) contended. 'People on both sides are dying, and it's our job to convey that truth in simple human terms. The Net has done that magnificently.' Critics, for their part, were yet to be persuaded. 'The myth of the Internet war, media's latest over-hyped theme about the Net, was as widespread as it was wrong', argued Jon Katz (1999b) of *Wired*. 'If the war in Kosovo demonstrates anything about the Net, it shows that it's a dreadful medium for covering a war.' In his view, the important reporting was provided by conventional – not digital – media. That is to say, while digital journalism offered interesting stories, it was the traditional war correspondents associated with major news organizations that produced the coverage that had a significant impact on the conduct of the war and its perception by the public. Nevertheless, and herein lies the rub, this conventional reporting was itself sadly wanting. In offering an appraisal of its limitations, Katz (1999a) highlighted what he considered to be a misguided sense of news values. 'The legacy of the Monica Lewinsky [scandal] hovers eerily over news media and the rest of the country' as it attempted to comprehend the 'confusing and horrifying images coming out of Serbia and Kosovo', he wrote shortly after the NATO bombing commenced.

In arguing that the Clinton administration's preoccupation with the sexual scandal severely hampered its capacity to handle the crisis in Kosovo (a scandal co-produced by 'journalists and members of the Republican Party'), Katz maintained that this neglect was engendered, in part, by irresponsible journalistic obsessions with a 'private sexual relationship that, just a few weeks since impeachment, seems almost incomprehensively trivial and significant'. As a result, he suggested, it is hardly surprising that the majority of US citizens were unable to understand the nature of the crisis in Kosovo, where it came from, or how it might be resolved. In his words:

> Even as people struggle to absorb the implications of the Techno-War, and to try and grasp the complex history of the region, they are stunned by the awful realities of Kosovo. By the captured soldiers, the maimed civilians, the tortured faces of so many refugees. Even as they are being asked to prepare themselves for a long, costly, and potentially bloody sacrifice, the public is still struggling to figure out how this nightmare came to be. (Katz, 1999a)

The arrogance demonstrated by journalism, when coupled with confusion about its purpose, had led to a 'disconnection' from its public that was profoundly dangerous, in his view. There was every reason to believe, it followed, that the conflict would have turned out differently had it been covered properly from the outset. 'In Kosovo we're seeing the very real consequences of journalism's twisted modern agenda, and of a poorly served public', he wrote. 'Kosovo shows us every night on the evening news what a big story really is, and just how dreadful the damage can be when journalists can no longer tell the difference.'

Criticisms of a different sort were levelled by Brooke Shelby Biggs, news editor of the MoJo.wire. In expressing her deep scepticism about the quality of the online coverage, she argued that insufficient care had been taken to differentiate news from propaganda. Pointing to several of the more celebrated examples of 'amateur' reporting discussed above, she contended:

> [I]n place of real reporting, we're offered a flood of unmediated dispatches from nonjournalists often with a personal interest in how the war is fought and how it ends. NPR features the impossibly sympathetic Albanian Kosovar teenager; Salon offers us the self-righteous Serbian citizens (with disclaimer). Wired News publicized the 'cyber-monk' of Kosovo. CNN is branding its Kosovo e-mail regurgitation as 'In-Depth.' This isn't really news, it's hearsay. But because we have no truly reliable sources of news on Kosovo, responsible journalists are looking to the Net to recruit Yugoslavs as amateur correspondents. These people have no ethical mandate to be unbiased any more than the government of Yugoslavia or the U.S. Defense Department does. (Biggs, 1999)

For Biggs, many online journalists are so committed to the idea of the internet as a 'great tool of the truth' that they overlook the possibility that 'man-on-the-street analysis' may itself he tainted with misinformation. The presumption that ordinary people's voices are independent needs to be questioned anew. Proper investigative reporting, it follows, must not be displaced by 'straight from the source' features believed to be objective. To the extent that this has happened, Biggs maintained, reporters have shirked their duty to verify and contextualize the statements of their sources. The consequence, she concluded, is that '[we] remove ourselves from accountability. And in so doing, we ultimately damage the legitimacy of Internet-borne news.'

Deep misgivings about the consequences engendered by the driving imperative of 'real-time' immediacy shaping digital war reporting – whether on television or the internet – were expressed by members of the military as well. 'With the explosion of 24-hour news outlets, there's greater pressure not only to report in real time, before facts can be evaluated and confirmed – but then those often factually unreliable stories are instantly dissected, analyzed, and commented upon on the air', one senior military public affairs officer insisted. 'The irony is that this environment of 24-hour news coverage and "talking-heads" programming is creating more heat, but less and less illumination' (cited in Kitfield, 1999). Moreover, throughout the conflict, fears were expressed by some officials that live reporting – 'war on television as it happens' – was providing Serbian authorities with information of considerable use to them in military terms. Digital media, it followed, would have to be countered by a more restrictive policy being adopted, according to a Pentagon spokesperson, Kenneth Bacon:

> We now live in an era where information is made available instantly to the enemy. We know that they watch television. We know that they are on the Internet. We know that they have cell phones. They are watching planes take off from airports all across Europe, and they can calculate the time it takes them to get to their targets, and they can calibrate their air defenses. So we want to give the enemy as little information as we can in order to help them with their own defenses against the attacks. (Transcript, NewsHour with Jim Lehrer, 6 April 1999)

To the extent that 'real-time' reporting was perceived to pose risks for 'operational security', efforts to 'manage' it were justified from a military perspective. Certainly there was little doubt in the minds of officials that winning the military campaign necessitated securing a victory in the media campaign at the same time. Their frustration in this regard was palpable. Admiral James Ellis, for example, observed that 'the enemy was much better at this [public information and public affairs (PA)] than we were . . . and far more nimble.' Serbian successes in getting their preferred message into circulation contrasted favourably with NATO's difficulties in countering it. 'The enemy deliberately and criminally killed innocents by the thousands, but no one saw it', he insisted. 'We accidentally killed innocents, sometimes by the dozens, and the world watched on the evening news. We were continuously reacting, investigating, and trying to answer "how could this happen?"' (cited in Pounder, 2000: 58).

Responses to this and related lines of criticism were often met by journalists convinced that 'information management' represented press manipulation in a different guise. It was alleged that NATO officials' steadfast refusal to acknowledge mistakes – until succumbing to intense pressure from the press – seriously undermined their credibility. Contradictory statements, when identified as such by angry journalists, routinely put officials on the defensive. Examples of such incidents – including the mistaken attack launched against two civilian convoys near the village of Djakovica – followed a familiar pattern, they maintained, whereby NATO denials and obfuscation would eventually give way as contrary evidence accumulated. Such attempts to 'manage' journalists, it followed, undermined trust – and, as such, ultimately proved counter-productive for the military. 'NATO couldn't get its own story straight', Michael Hirsh (1999) of Newsweek commented with regard to the Djakovica atrocity, pointing out that Supreme Commander Wesley Clark's contention that the Serbs were responsible for the civilian casualties was irresponsible. 'In the end', he concluded, 'NATO hurt its credibility far more than Milosevic did.' Efforts to shore up this credibility, and in so doing regain the moral high ground, included a reorganization of NATO's Media Operations Centre (MOC), conducted by Alastair Campbell, Tony Blair's press secretary, in the aftermath of Djakovica. In explaining his conviction that 'it was vital to try to hold the public's interest on our terms', Campbell (1999) implemented a number of changes, including a policy whereby NATO mistakes would be acknowledged but the ultimate blame for them would be placed squarely on the Milošević government. Critics such as Knightley (2004) pointed out that the 'dubious reasoning' behind Campbell's policy meant that, 'if Milosevic had not forced Nato to resort to bombing to bring him to heel, then Nato bombers would not have made mistakes and civilians would not have been killed.' In other words, he added, by 'the same sort of logic, Ho Chi Minh was responsible for the American atrocity at My Lai' (2004: 513).

A further line of criticism, often implied in the cases discussed above, pointed to the ways in which audience expectations had been heightened by digital technologies. 'People have gotten very used to live news, and that makes us have to go places and transmit live', stated Marcy McGinnis at CBS News in New York. 'There's a lot of pressure to be somewhere immediately, and in that sense I do get more nervous than I did in the past', she added. 'You get people on a plane and then you think, "Oh, my God, we've put them in the middle of a bombing campaign." Today, technology makes it possible for us to go places and be in situations that are inherently more dangerous' (cited in Littlefield, 1999). Compounding this pressure was the perception that this public desire for real-time dispatches was intensifying to the point that it was becoming a problem in and of itself, with harmful consequences. 'Television in particular is a medium that allows people at home to become violence voyeurs', stated Ted Koppel, host of ABC's 'Nightline'. 'The more they see, the more it takes to gain their interest the next day.' Moreover, he maintained, 'it's all happening so fast and such an enormous volume is being churned out, that people become very jaded by what they see very quickly' (cited in Barringer, 1999). Evidently what digital media's advocates considered to be a virtue afforded by new technologies – that is, that such reporting was to be valued for the way in which it could involve or engage the viewer, effectively allowing them to see for themselves what was happening – was, for critics, evidence of undue influence distorting the nature of the coverage itself. Digital technology, it followed, was a 'double-edged sword', as Nick Pollard, head of news at Sky Television at the time, observed in his appraisal of its relative strengths and limitations. 'You have to make sure you give your journalists time to be journalists', he concluded. 'Being live for the sake of being live is a pretty hollow achievement' (cited in Barber, 1999).

In the next chapter, we turn to the US-led wars in Afghanistan and Iraq, where we explore the features of a digital media landscape that is similar in many respects, yet markedly different in others. News organizations have continued to recraft their use of the technologies of satellite dish, videophone, laptop and cell phone to present viewers with a flood of stories and images from the battlefield. Some of the ensuing coverage has confronted distant publics with the consequences of high explosives and bullets, while some of it has effectively sanitized death into a pixellated spectacle. An important theme in our discussion is that, while certain hard lessons were learned from Kosovo – by journalists and officials alike – others, tragically, were not.

CHAPTER THREE

Conflicted Realities

Introduction

On 13 November 2001, the Afghan capital of Kabul lay before the US-allied Northern Alliance troops. As the forces regrouped before entering the city, and as the defeated Taliban troops and officials fled their posts, a small group of journalists, led by the BBC's John Simpson, marched towards the city. Crowds of Kabul residents greeted them as they walked along the main road heading for the Hotel Intercontinental in the middle of town. 'I grabbed as many hands as I could, laughing with the relief and pleasure of it all', Simpson later wrote. 'To be the first journalists out of so many to enter the most closed and difficult city on earth: it was a superb moment' (Simpson, 2002). Caught up in the emotion, Simpson delivered a piece to camera, stating: 'It was only BBC people who liberated this city. We got in ahead of Northern Alliance troops' (BBC, 2001). The moment captures both the sense of opportunity and the hubris surrounding the communication technology used in both Afghanistan and Iraq. Simpson and his colleagues could now report from nearly anywhere on the battlefield, taking viewers to the front with apparent ease. In doing so, however, they risked becoming even more deeply implicated as actors shaping the conduct of the war than reporters in Kosovo had been two years earlier. Digital technology had placed the journalist nearly centre stage (not quite centre stage, because the new technology of the camera phone failed to deliver, meaning that the piece was not in the end live television) for better or, – in the view of some – for worse.

This chapter is about journalists' use of these communications tools during these conflicts, technologies which CNN president Chris Cramer called 'the true newscaster's dream', because they allow journalists to 'bring news, as it happens, from anywhere in the globe' (Cramer, 2004). The story of journalism, we will suggest, involves much more than reciting a list of technological advances towards a clearer, more vivid picture of the realities of conflict. For many commentators, the capacity to relay a proliferation of voices and of images from the battle zones simply amplified the propaganda war. The excited voices of correspondents accompanying US soldiers in tanks rushing towards Baghdad in March 2003 were, one of those correspondents reflected later, 'the best propaganda' for the US government (Gottleib, 2003). As the campaign continued, video of Sunni fighters firing mortars or exploding roadside mines under passing US military vehicles, beamed across Iraq by the pirate satellite television channel Al Zawraa, were widely read as a propaganda victory for those opposing the US occupation (Roggio, 2006). At the same time, personal blogs or digital cameras were being used by others to give access to previously marginalized voices and to open up new ways of understanding the conflicts. The website Life in Baghdad, for example, provided global audiences with powerful images, shot by Iraqis, of everyday life under the US occupation, when few Western journalists dared to work in the city.

At issue in these diverse accounts is the oft-repeated claim that digital technology creates a more accurate or truthful mode of reporting, one capable of evading censorship while simultaneously offering a heightened sense of immediacy from the war zone. The story of journalism during these wars becomes, in part, a story of the search for technologies which will render the conduct of war in greater clarity and experiential depth than ever before (discourses of technology's liberating power, heard in Kosovo, being ever more pronounced). Moreover, this is a story about how the increasing centrality of technologies of mediation in the fighting of 'new wars' (detailed in chapter 1) offers opportunities – but also poses threats – in the ongoing struggle to secure spaces for independent journalism to flourish.

The chapter begins with a consideration of two prominent, contrasting uses of new technology in the mediation of the 2001–2 phase of the US war against the Taliban in Afghanistan: the reliance on digital simulations of an otherwise largely invisible bombing campaign and the mobility accorded to correspondents on the ground in the country by satellite phone. It then takes up the themes of a highly mobile, accelerated journalism in consideration of the spectacular Western coverage of the US-led invasion of Iraq in 2003, coverage which was very soon severely criticized for its inaccuracy and its reproduction of a military gaze. Consideration then turns to the emergence during the Iraq War of blogs and other personal media as tools of reporting. In a significant challenge to established modes of mediating war, subjective and experiential forms of reporting, among which the blog is most prominent, gained status. Here the relationship between journalist and audience was being actively renegotiated, at times in surprising ways.

Afghanistan: representing an invisible war

The search for technology-driven solutions to the longstanding problem of how to render war dispassionately and fairly was already evident in the reporting of the US aerial bombing of Afghanistan in 2001 and 2002, but came to the fore in the days leading up to the ground war between US-backed and Taliban-allied forces. This war was a relatively closed affair. Very few journalists – a handful from major broadcasters such as the BBC and Al Jazeera and from news agencies – were licensed by the Taliban government to work in the country before the bombing started, and most of those were evicted as war loomed. The US and allied forces, in turn, gave few journalists access to their operations, which largely comprised long-range bombing sorties and secretive special operations campaigns, and sought to control other information flows as well. *The Guardian* in Britain reported that the Pentagon sought to buy up commercial satellite images of the country to reduce the visual evidence of the effects of bombing being seen in the West (Campbell, 2001). Much of the 'on the ground' reporting actually came from Pakistan and relied on official accounts from both sides, augmented by refugee testimony. Unclear, among other details, was how many civilians died in the first waves of US bombing sorties (later estimated by non-governmental groups at 1,000 to 1,300 people; Conetta, 2002).

Digital reporting tools of two kinds became prominent in this context. Information graphics and other technologies of simulation took on new importance to represent the otherwise unseen conflict. News websites, in particular, established their point of difference to print and broadcast partly through such graphics. CBS, for example, provided what it called 'interactive maps' on its news site in which users could zoom in on and pan around satellite images of pre-war Kabul, Kandahar and a Taliban camp called Darunta, down to the detail of cave entrances or planes on runways (BusinessWire, 2001). These tended to do so in narrow ways, often reproducing official and, in particular, military-sanctioned versions of what was happening in the war. No sustained effort was made to inform news consumers about the capability of munitions such as the 'daisy cutter' bombs dropped in the Tora Bora gorge (at 15,000 lb, reputedly some of the largest conventional bombs ever used) to kill large numbers of the Taliban and demoralize survivors. Neat red stars, for example, signified explosions, and arrows indicated the shock waves that would overwhelm soldiers sheltering in caves in ways that were clearly deeply reductive of the effects of war. Vujakovic (2002: 192) notes that information graphics often work 'as guarantor and visual confirmation of the ability of "our" forces to hit the right targets'. He describes graphics and maps as important sites of knowledge creation during war – during the 1999 Kosovo conflict, 167 maps of the region were published in five UK newspapers in one month alone (ibid.: 190). As Wark (1994: 71; also Walsh and Barbara, 2006) notes, audiences are placed in these images intertextually somewhere between military planners and computer-game players, reducing the distance required for critical responses to the war and making the suffering of those on the ground invisible, and thereby simulating at the same time an audience consensus in favour of triumphant US military power. Graphics were arguably still more important in Afghanistan, where news organizations were unable to film the bombing of Kabul or access contemporary satellite footage. As the propaganda war heated up ahead of the US invasion of Iraq in 2003, such ideologically loaded graphics reappeared. CNN's website, for example, provided detailed illustrations of Iraq's suspected arsenal of chemical and biological weapons (see Seib, 2003: 627) – a central justification for the war. In graphic form, these hypothesized weapons took on solid form, something they were never to do in actuality. Similarly, Spain's *El Mundo*, which made heavy use of interactive graphics on its website, provided a map of the Middle East on which users could move around missile launchers, with rings rippling out from them, to see how far Iraq's Al Hussein rockets might reach. Left out was important information such as the unreliability of these weapons, or UN estimates that, while Iraq fired about 1,000 of them in the 1991 war, it had 'around a dozen' left by late 2002 (Sengupta, 2002).

The second major digital technology we wish to highlight in the reporting of the Afghanistan war, the satellite phone – and its accompanying technology, the videophone – stands at the heart of major changes in war reporting and in journalism's relations with combatants and governments. The videophone had proven its dramatic value to journalism on 31 December 1999, when CNN had for the first time broadcast video of a breaking news story using a video camera connected to a satellite uplink unit that digitized the signal and sent it through an Inmarsat satellite phone. The story – incidentally also in Afghanistan – concerned the hijacking of an Air India jet by Muslim Kashmiri separatists. CNN's Eli Flournoy recalled the jerky 6-frames-per-second images coming into Atlanta:

> All of a sudden, one of the cockpit windows opened up and men began to climb out. CNN carried the hijacking's dramatic conclusion LIVE on all its networks, domestic and international,

with Nic Robertson narrating the escape of the hijackers and their freed Kashmiri compatriots, and the safe release of the remaining hostages from the plane. (Flournoy, 2003)

Mobile communications technologies allowed journalists to report live with much greater ease from any location on the globe. They also appeared to afford greater independence from military or political control. In late 2001, as the Taliban forces retreated or disbanded under the US bombing onslaught, a wave of reporters equipped with portable digital satellite phones crossed from Pakistan, with sixty soon based in Jalalabad close to the border. From there, *The Independent*'s Richard Lloyd Parry was able to report, within hours of the US's denial that its planes had done so, the destruction of the village of Kamo Ado in early December 2001 and the deaths of an estimated 115 people (Parry, 2001). Without satellite phones, fewer news organizations would have sent reporters into a country where there was next to no civil international telephone system that could get the story out in a timely way (see GIPI-AF, 2006). Parry called the satellite phone 'the most essential and closely guarded item . . . without which the most astonishing news story is useless' (ibid.), while one commentator described Afghanistan as 'the first videophone war' (Wasserman, 2001).

Portable communications such as these breathed new life into the tradition of the independent foreign correspondent. Reporters enjoyed a sense of validation in the role of speaking directly to audiences, over the heads of both editors and officials. While still restricted in their movements by military on both sides during the months of war, they were much more mobile than reporters had been just a few years earlier – the latter having been restricted, when reporting live, to delivering their material from hotel roofs, surrounded by technicians and equipment often weighing a tonne. By 2007, freelancer Vaughan Smith, who accompanied the British Grenadier Guards on deployment in Helmand province, Afghanistan, could travel with no more telecommunications equipment than an Apple MacBook Pro laptop, a compact satellite phone and two portable video cameras.

He contrasted the technology of nine years previously: 'I recall taking 16 heavy boxes down to Pristina in the spring of 1998, just to film and edit and not feed. I can't now imagine what was in them' (Smith, 2007). In addition to being mobile, reporting was much more frequently live, privileging the dramatic image of the journalist in the midst of conflict as 'authentic' testimony.

Yet, at the same time, reporters were on occasion situated slightly differently through this technology of immediacy. The BBC's Simpson and Jouvenal were criticized by colleagues for becoming the story, not only for their 'liberation of Kabul' but for a ruse a month before. Hidden under burqas, they had smuggled themselves over the Afghan border to deliver a hushed live 'piece to cam' via videophone from within sight of a Taliban watch post (Simpson, 2002: 175ff.). The technology also failed to work that time and the report had to be taped and sent a day later, but the BBC's most senior foreign correspondent was clearly adapting to the availability of new tools, in part by refashioning his relationship of trust with distant audiences. This technology of liveness cast journalists as actors in war, acting out their independence and intrepidness for audiences who could follow them in near-real time (reminiscent, in some ways, of how war reports from Baghdad hotel roofs made CNN's reputation in 1991). The live, mobile report from the war zone, with its pixellated images and distorted sound, sustained an epistemological claim to speak directly from the reality of war. One producer argued:

> The technology has progressed to the point that it allows the viewer to see more of the process of gathering news . . . People are seeing news as it develops. And I'm not sure that's bad. It kind of hits at some of the criticism of the media for slanting the news. You can't say it was slanted when it was live. (Cited in Seib, 2001: 44)

The situation was of course much more complicated than this discourse of technologically enabled freedom suggests. Tom Rosenstiel pointed out that one of the main reasons the US military was nervous about providing journalists with access to the front was because of this combination of liveness with mobility,

Communications equipment became significantly smaller, cheaper
and more portable between the first Gulf War and the invasion of
Iraq. The low mobility of this CBS TV crew at a hotel in Dahran,
Saudi Arabia, in 1991 (top) provides a sharp contrast with that of Getty
Images photographer Joe Raedle, embedded with a forward column
of US Marines in April 2003 (bottom). © AFP (top); © Getty Images
(bottom)

leading them to place much greater emphasis on managed briefings in Washington. As a result, he observes, 'a great deal more of what we consider war coverage today occurs in the Pentagon press briefing room' (cited in Campbell, 2001). In an ironic twist, Campbell (2001) observes in this regard, 'reporters can deliver news from war zones in real time, but they have less to tell.' As we explore below, technology was being routinely singled out as a source of tension between journalists and their minders.

Journalism of the sightline

Iraq was a war covered, at least in its initial 'spectacular' phase, by extraordinary numbers of journalists, equipped with a wider range of communication tools than had been seen in any previous war. At the outbreak of the invasion, news organizations sent 4,000 foreign correspondents, among them 700 accepting the US and UK governments' invitation to 'embed' themselves with military units, including front-line troops. These reporters carried satellite phones, higher quality videophones, laptops, digital cameras and night-vision cameras. One reporter, NBC's David Bloom, even brought with him a $500,000 tank recovery vehicle, modified to be able to transmit television-quality video to a satellite while driving at 100 km/h. Bloom's effort – aside from the enormous expenditure – was typical in seeking to use technology 'to tell the soldier's story and to bring the realities of war home to the American people live as it happened' (Melanie Bloom, cited in Reid, 2007). Technology was lauded for compressing the distance between Western living rooms and the experiences of soldiers at war.

In addition to television's enhanced claim to immediacy, web-based journalism was expanding significantly during the invasion. Berenger (2006) cites figures suggesting that US and UK news organization websites attracted between 30 and 150 per cent more visits in the first two weeks of the invasion of Iraq in March 2003, with the BBC's site alone receiving 150 million visits. More significant for other commentators – particularly given the dominance of television as the news medium of choice for most people at the time – were new features developed by newsrooms. The widespread availability of broadband internet in many Western countries, combined with competition between news organizations eager to make use of the long run-up to war to enhance their online provision, led to what Palser (2003) called a 'cornucopia of creative and experimental presentation formats'. These included multimedia resources, among them more richly interactive maps and slide shows, as well as new video services (such as Reuters' raw videos from the field that contained no voiceover) and blog diaries from journalists. Palser cites the enthusiasm of many journalists and editors for the potential of web-based and other digital reporting tools to extend their reach to audiences.

The 'explosion of information', as one BBC reporter called it (BBC, 2003: 2), ensuing from the combination of these communications technologies, together with the embedding of reporters with troops, has been widely criticized, however. Some have complained about the poor (albeit visually compelling) quality of reports, while others condemned what they perceive to be propagandist assumptions underpinning the claims made. Within days, observers were noticing that some embedded journalists appeared to be providing a decidedly narrow narrative in telling the war from the GI's point of view, and that breathless reports from the front line were sometimes inaccurate, in part because these reporters had little access to the wider picture. 'Talk about the "fog of war"', commented one such 'embed', M. L. Lyke of the *Seattle Post-Intelligencer*, on her blog. 'We're in the thick of it, knowing precious little' (Lyke, 2003). Lyke was aboard a US aircraft carrier where a mere two hours' worth of media briefings had been given that week. Mitchell (2003) recorded fifteen widely reported stories in the conflict's first week that were wrong, including the frequent misreporting of the taking of the first key Iraqi town, the port of Umm Qasr. The former BBC correspondent Martin Bell derided the coverage as the reporting of 'breaking rumour rather than breaking news' (Bell, 2003; see also Allan and Zelizer, 2004: 5). Moreover, the constantly open communication channel between the newsroom and the reporter in the field made the spectacle of reporting a somewhat empty one at times. 'Let's be perfectly candid about this', the ABC's Ted Koppel, broadcasting live from the Iraqi desert, told anchor Peter Jennings on one occasion when asked about the broader picture of the war. 'We get much of our news either when we chat with you or when we listen . . . to the BBC on shortwave on the hour' (cited in Boyer, 2003).

'Liveness' was overrated and overused. News channels in particular led a trend away from news packages towards live reports during the war. The Project for Excellence in Journalism calculated that 62 per cent of reports from Iraq shown on US news channels in 2004 were in live mode: 'In doing so', it argued, cable news 'has de-emphasized the story package's strengths, namely the chance to verify, edit and carefully choose words and pictures. The stress in cable news is on immediacy and cost efficiency of the live interview and unedited reporter stand-up' (PEJ, 2005). Seib's concerns, expressed a few years before, were prescient: by going live, broadcast and web-based news outlets 'give up the time that was a friend to judgment' (2001: xi). Nevertheless, the commitment to liveness found its defenders, who pointed to the different strengths it brought to the package. Immediacy compresses time and space so that viewers experience something of what the journalist experiences. CNN international news editor Eli Flournoy described the live video coming in from roving satellite-dish-equipped reporting teams in the following terms:

> Having live moving pictures lent an almost voyeuristic quality to the war coverage. The fascination of watching in on the exploration of the unknown, not knowing what story, or danger, lay ahead, through the capabilities of the satellite tracking videophone dish, was an experience shared by reporters, those of us at headquarters in Atlanta and viewers alike. (Flournoy, 2003)

Viewers appeared to like this coverage, with news channels attracting significantly higher audiences in March and April

2003. On the web, too, editors at Reuters, which provided 'raw video' from correspondents without commentary or final editing on its website, or at MSNBC.com, which streamed a webcam of the Baghdad skyline as the city was bombed, reported significant numbers of viewers simply leaving the sites open all day on their work computers (Palser, 2003). In removing some of broadcast journalism's usual packaging, such forms of coverage appealed as a step beyond immediate news to become, at least in appearance, unmediated or unfiltered news.

It must be emphasized that technologies of immediacy, while removing some news packaging, did not remove newsroom control. It became easier for journalists to file stories (as easy, MSNBC editor-in-chief Dean Wright commented, as if they were still in New York; Swartz, 2003), but also easier for editors to manage and instruct reporters. Anne Garrels, a correspondent for the US National Public Radio, reported being asked to redo her coverage of the toppling of the statue of Saddam Hussein in Baghdad's Firdos Square on 9 April 2003 because she was not reporting the celebrating crowds which the television networks were showing live (CJR, 2006: 21). At times journalists appeared to drift towards being extensions of their equipment, leaving editorial decisions to the office. Thus one embedded photographer, Cheryl Diaz Meyer of the *Dallas Morning News*, talked of being too tired to sort through her images of the invasion, which she tended to send, via her laptop and satellite connection, to her editors for them to deal with (Sylvester and Huffman, 2005: 93). Overall, it appeared that the ease of communication through these technologies exacerbated the trend towards the use of 'parachute' reporters, too many of whom were without the benefit of prior experience as war correspondents, let alone having any familiarity with the region itself. Some of these 'instant war reporters' struggled against the odds, having little of the correspondent's trade knowledge in how to negotiate stories through petty officials, recalcitrant telephone operators or patchy telecommunications systems. Cheaper and easier to use newsgathering technologies have hastened the decline of the specialist conflict news agency, some would argue, along with the expertise of their reporters (see Loyn, 2005).

Journalists themselves have often foregrounded their own views about how new technologies have influenced the reporting from Iraq. *San Jose Mercury News* reporter Dana Hull, for example, echoed Parry's experience in Afghanistan that the increasingly mobile journalist witnessing from the war zone was better able to assess the accuracy of reports from officials and from other media than those located at a distance or restricted to official press conferences (Hull, 2004: 133). Others cited technology as affording them a welcome degree of independence from military censors. When Chris Hondros of the photo agency Getty Images photographed a unit of soldiers mistakenly shooting a family driving home in the northern Iraqi town of Tal Afar, killing the parents in the front seats, he was able to convince a low-ranking officer to let him send haunting pictures of the newly orphaned, traumatized children to New York on his satellite phone that night. By the time a higher ranking officer, who wanted the images held until the army could investigate the incident, woke up the next morning, they were already on news websites (Hondros, cited in CJR, 2006: 74–8). Such stories abound within the journalism community. Yet, the overall assessment is unavoidable that the most expensive gadgets, particularly when combined with the relative inexperience of many of the flood of reporters sent to cover the invasion (and the embedding of some with troops in a 'patriotic climate'), in particular, could be as easily used to give a decidedly one-sided view of conflict. To Wall (2005: 112), 'issues of life and death can become sensationalized, trivialized and overshadowed by an obsession with high technology' (see also Thussu, 2003). Certainly, almost entirely eclipsed in coverage were problems that later became very apparent. Almost no Western journalists – or indeed soldiers – spoke the language of the country in which they were operating. Moreover, the relentless stream of images sidelined questions about the morality, let alone legality, of the invasion, or about the validity of claims that Iraq posed a military threat to the West.

Cultural theorist Paul Virilio's metaphor of the sightline is useful in critiquing the way journalism became caught up in particular relationships with technology during the invasion of Iraq. Virilio argues that technology's promise of allowing us to see 'better' is deeply reductive. In particular, he traces many of the technologies of speed and visual media back to solutions to military problems, which he sees as enslaving contemporary culture to a 'faith in the technical sightline' and reducing the visual to the 'line of a sighting device' (Virilio, 1994: 13; see also Armitage, 1999). Crandall (2005) likewise points to the similarities between military 'operational media' and news media. Operational media, a term which includes both simulations that enable battle plans to be role played and technologies that allow control centres to see via the soldier's equipment, are explicitly designed to reduce the time taken to think or reflect - time that could otherwise lose the soldier his or her life. In Crandall's view, 'real-time' media slip towards this military world, inserting the public into the position of the pilot in his or her cockpit or the soldier in his or her green night-vision goggles, and removing the time that journalists and the public need to reflect and put events into context (Crandall, 2005: 7–8).

Hindsight does indeed suggest that it was often what we might call 'slow journalists', reporters who eschewed the embeds and the high-tech communications technology, who were best able to construct accounts of the invasion and occupation of Iraq which extended beyond the messages propagated by politicians. Dexter Filkins of the *New York Times*, who lingered behind the front lines to interview locals in the newly 'liberated' town of Safwan in southern Iraq, was one of the first Western reporters to note how suspicious and traumatized these people were. He observed 'the immensity of the job that still awaits the allies' (Filkins, 2003). As a number of studies have documented (including PEJ, 2003; Rafeeq, 2007; Walsh and Barbara, 2006), there was a dearth of such analytical journalism during the invasion, a problem compounded by the near absence of images of death or injury, particularly in reports from embeds. Despite the huge quantity of news material sent out of Iraq and the illusion that the war was being seen live in its totality, much was unreported. One US correspondent reflected later on some of the gaps in the coverage, particularly the elision of Iraqis' own views about being invaded: 'I think a lot of us picked up on the very first day [of the taking of Baghdad] a lot of very ambivalent feelings, and those feelings were basically completely overwhelmed by the images and, most important, the superficial event that took place that day – the statue [of Saddam Hussein in Firdos Square] being taken down, the Americans taking control of the city' (cited in CJR, 2006: 20–1). The spectacle of real-time war constructed by journalists and the military was not only a partial and inaccurate picture, but it marginalized alternative perspectives of the war.

Relevant here is a concern expressed by visual culture scholars, namely that entertainment conventions, drawn from patriotic US films as well as video games, overpowered other ways of seeing, particularly in the televisual representations of the invasion of Iraq. Andersen (2006) argues, for example, that films such as *Black Hawk Down* (2001), a visually realistic (if factually flawed) account of the US military operation in Somalia in 1993, in which viewers could share a visceral sense of war from the perspective of the US Rangers, came to stand as the authentic version of war and therefore as a model for reporting actual wars. The realism of the film, with its 'almost tactile sense of the conflict – the dust of the streets, the reports of the guns, the agony as bullets rip into flesh, the taste of sweat, blood and grime' (Galber, 2002) – allowed US audiences to celebrate the heroism of individual soldiers and to see war in terms of their experience, eliding away any political or moral considerations. Andersen cites a number of commentators who noted the deep similarities to the film's script, visual effects and even dialogue in the highly successful propaganda film released by the Pentagon to news organizations concerning the alleged 'saving' of Private Jessica Lynch from a Nasiriyah hospital in the second week of the invasion of Iraq. *Time* magazine, for example, quoted one officer pleased that the rescue 'worked perfectly. It was like Black Hawk Down except nothing went wrong' (cited in Andersen, 2006: 238). In fact, as a BBC documentary was to show a month later, the story of Lynch's rescue was more fiction than reality, but it had a significant impact on public support in the US for the war nonetheless. Such direct parallels were rare, and one must emphasize the ideological climate more than representational conventions in shaping the extent to which audiences interpreted the Iraq war coverage in terms of expectations derived from popular films. But a digital aesthetic is perhaps shared across entertainment and television news genres, allowing highly selective and ideologically motivated accounts to define the reality of war. To an extent, journalism was in danger of becoming another branch of what a number of scholars have termed 'militainment' (Andersen, 2006; see also Der Derian's 2001 conception of the military–industrial–media–entertainment network).

The critique of a militarized Western culture connects with some journalists' own concerns about the extent to which their reporting has become subsumed within a wider information war. As discussed in chapter 1, communications technologies have taken on greater importance in military strategy, with some planners talking of the need for 'total information dominance'. The desire to control journalism has increased as a consequence. Here we wish to underscore the degree to which journalism has at the same time become increasingly politicized, particularly in the Middle East, where Western-style objectivity is open to challenge, and where there has been a growth in politically partisan media (from US-funded propaganda sheets in Baghdad (Gerth and Shane, 2005) to Hezbollah-funded Al Manar TV in Lebanon). It was not just in Taliban-ruled Afghanistan, then, that 'the assumption that correspondents are more useful as witnesses than as targets' (Bennett, cited in Foerstel, 2006: 21) has been proved sadly unfounded. Allan and Zelizer (2004) talk of an overall change in the 'rules of engagement' for journalism. In this context, journalists have become increasingly vulnerable to attack, with more dying in Iraq than in any conflict since the Second World War. By October 2008, Reporters sans frontières reported 223 journalists and media assistants killed in the five years since the war began, many of them Iraqi nationals employed by local and international media – compared with fifty-five killed in twenty years of conflict in Vietnam (RSF, 2008).

While individual cases of the deaths of journalists in Iraq are contested, the bigger picture is clearer. Along with the rearticulation of war correspondence as live or near-live reporting through the technologies of portable satellite, cell phone and computer has come a much greater vulnerability for the journalist. When no longer perceived to be a neutral observer, the war correspondent is at grave risk of becoming regarded as a combatant. Examples abound: when John Simpson entered Kabul ahead of the US-backed Northern Alliance, or Brent Sadler of CNN broadcast live his foray, in a satellite-equipped four-wheel drive, in March 2003 into Tikrit ahead of US troops (see Levinson, 2004: 145), they were broadcasting what was tactical military information in a battle still taking place. This intensification of existing tensions between journalists and military analysts, expressed already by both parties during the Kosovo war, grew more heated as the number of deaths among journalists rose. BBC World presenter Nik Gowing argued that the intrusiveness of real-time reporting into the field of war had turned journalists into targets:

> The new, insidious development is that because of the impact of our real-time capability to bear witness immediately, we are being actively targeted by warriors, warlords and forces of even the most highly developed governments who do not want us to see what they are doing. This is the price of the new technological advances that we journalists can now use to work in conflicts. (Gowing, 2003: 232–3)

Embedding with forces was supposed to reduce that risk, in exchange for some limitations on movement. However, a third of the reporters that the Committee to Protect Journalists (CPJ) listed as killed in 2003 were embedded with US troops at the time (CPJ, 2003). Many, although not the CPJ, concluded that it was hard to construe the killing by US forces of a number of journalists in the war's first months, including ITN's Terry Lloyd,

Al Jazeera's Tareq Ayoub, Telecinco's José Couso, and Reuters' Taras Protsyuk and Mazen Dana, as simply accidental. The bombing of Al Jazeera and Abu Dhabi TV offices in Baghdad on 8 April raised further concerns, leading Al Jazeera correspondent Majed Abdel Hadi to accuse the US of dragging journalists into the conflict: 'We were targeted because the Americans don't want the world to see the crimes they are committing against the Iraqi people' (Al Jazeera, 2003). At best the attacks appeared to be evidence of a greatly reduced concern for journalists' personal safety. When CNN chief news executive Eason Jordan expressed a similar sentiment in February 2005, the uproar among right-wing bloggers (discussed further in chapter 4) forced him to leave his job. By late 2004, as the security situation in Baghdad deteriorated to the point where many Western journalists were unable to leave their heavily fortified offices (or the 'Green Zone', where military briefings were given), on-the-ground reporting was left largely to Iraqi nationals brave enough to risk summary execution by various contending forces. The high-tech coverage had largely ground to a halt.

Situated journalism

While the sense of liveness enabled by emerging technologies is central to many of the issues journalism continues to face during these conflicts, quite different uses of digital media are also to be found. On the internet a significant number of alternative forms of recording the conflict have evolved over recent years, many of them practised by individuals operating outside the main institutions of the news. Whether it was *The Independent* reporter Robert Fisk's collection of unpublishable images of the horrific impact of war on civilians (www.robert-fisk.com) or the e-mailed reports from a US major in Afghanistan published on Glenn Reynolds's blog (www.instapundit.com), these forms extended beyond existing conventions of war reporting in sometimes dramatic ways. One form in particular, the blog, came to prominence in the initial phase of the Iraq War. Blogs were heralded for providing a

voice that appeared to some commentators distinctive in its ability to produce independent, immediate and insightful accounts of
what was actually happening on the ground. This led to a form of
witnessing of conflict in which the individual reporter acted less
as a cipher – or, more to the point, as a stenographer to power –
and more as the audience's technologically enhanced eyes and
ears. Rather than bringing the war into people's living rooms,
the blog went some way to taking people into the war zone.

Many of the most noteworthy blogs were produced by amateurs – that is, ordinary citizens temporarily assuming the role of
journalist. Salam Pax (the name being a pseudonym), an unem-
ployed Baghdad architect, provided embedded journalism of
a quite different order to that produced by reporters travelling
with US and allied forces. Salam's accounts of living in Baghdad
under the shadow of invasion, posted on his blog Where is Raed?
(dear_raed.blogspot.com), were interspersed with his angry
denunciations of both George W. Bush and Saddam Hussein.
It was his reportage of everyday life in the city, however, that
offered, as one commentator observed, 'an easy intimacy that
eludes the one-size-fits-all coverage of Baghdad's besieged residents' (Allemang, 2003). As Salam's blog was cited in discussion
groups, in other blogs and then in news columns, readership
reportedly grew to 20,000 (R. McCarthy, 2003). US journalist
Paul Andrews (2003) observed that his writings attracted interest
because they related the 'inside Baghdad' story of the war with
an authority and insight that reports from Western journalists
all too often lacked (indeed, he adds, journalists were often 'so
jingoistic and administration-friendly as to proscribe any sense
of impartiality or balance'). At the same time, blogs from the
perspectives of soldiers in Iraq were also attracting significant
readership and media attention. L. T. Smash promised 'unfiltered news' from a soldier's point of view through his blog In
the Sandbox, and claimed 6,000 hits a day at the blog's peak
in mid-2003. As invasion became occupation by 2004, Colby
Buzzell, a US soldier posted in Mosul, wrote posts to his blogs
that one reviewer called 'thrilling and raw reading, warfare nearly

instantaneously transfigured from memory to text' (Swofford, 2005). Hockenberry (2005) counted more than 100 of these 'milblogs' during the war's early months alone.

It became clear that the perceptive and vivid accounts of the better 'warblogs' posed a challenge for news organizations, particularly for those foreign correspondents accused of spending more time with each other in air-conditioned hotels than in interviewing civilians or those waging the conflict. Too often their observations, critics pointed out, appeared to be second hand and, in any case, lagging behind bloggers' accounts (Dodge, 2003). 'Riverbend', a young middle-class woman, like Salam Pax writing in English, reported neighbourhood rumours of ethnic cleansing in Baghdad's Shiite and Sunni suburbs before Western news outlets recognized the scale and intent of the killing. Frequently the criteria of good journalism being employed were shaped by bloggers' own ideological commitments for – or against – the waging of the conflict. Whatever one makes of particular blogs, Wall suggests that 'their embodiment of the notion that an amateur news fan with access to the Internet can become a sort of secondary war correspondent may well be the [2003] Gulf War bloggers' most significant contribution to journalism' (Wall, 2005: 122). The growing numbers of blogs also posed a threat to political and military control. Indeed, many Iraqi bloggers, among them Salam Pax and Riverbend, were forced to keep their identities secret for fear their lives were at risk. Meanwhile, a number of soldiers' blogs were closed down by their officers, among them Armor Geddon, an enthusiastically violent account of killing insurgents during the US campaign in Falluja in November 2004 (discussed further in the following chapter) which jarred with official statements that all care was being taken to safeguard civilians.

These para-journalistic forms, while a topic for underemployed journalists waiting for the Iraq invasion to begin and an increasingly significant source of news for the public, remained more or less on the margins of news reporting during the war's early stages. Only occasionally did they enter the news pages for the information they gathered or located, such as when blogger Raed Jarrar organized a house-to-house survey in Baghdad and southern Iraq to attempt to estimate the civilian casualties of the invasion (see www.civilians.info/iraq). Under the headline 'Iraq's secret daily death toll', the news agency Agence France Press quoted Jarrar criticizing the official silence on the number of dead: 'Neither the Iraqi government nor the American forces are interested in getting the exact figures' (Agence France Presse, 2004). As the next chapter explores, the status of citizen blogs changed to an extent as the war progressed, with Arab bloggers in particular – by some accounts numbering 100 within Iraq and over 1,000 across the Middle East within a few years of Salam's rise to fame – becoming, in one critic's words, 'a viable alternative to the heavily censored, state-run media' in many countries (Roasa, 2008). From the war's start, however, a small but significant group of journalists and news organizations began experimenting with the blog format, attracted by the emphasis on the independent and immediate observations of the writer. One significant long-term development which resulted from the Iraq War, then, was the incorporation of blogging within war journalism's set of tools.

In the case of freelancer Christopher Allbritton (formerly a reporter with the AP wire service and New York *Daily News*), the blog provided both the business and the communication model for a form of journalism which was unique. Allbritton had announced his intention to be the web's first independent war correspondent in the months leading up to the invasion. On a blog called Back to Iraq (www.back-to-iraq.com), he asked readers to help contribute to the financial support necessary to fund his travel and expenses to report on the looming conflict. Outlining his 'basic pitch' in the post 'Iraq or Bust', he explained to his readers:

> You get to read good reporting, thoughtful commentary and unique photographs (and video if I can hook up with some camera people). But as they say on late night television, 'There's more!'
> Not only do you get to contribute to a good cause, i.e.,

independent journalism, but the donors get put on a private email list. You will have access to stories, photos and raw notes – as well as personal observations – before the Web site or other media outlets do. You can also request stories to be covered. If you hear rumors of, say, guerilla fighting in Basra, ask me to check it out. If it's humanly possible and it's not a deathtrap, you get to play assignment editor! (Back to Iraq, 13 February 2003)

Allbritton was optimistic that he would be able to borrow a satellite telephone (a Motorola 9505), and that a new laptop would be donated. Contributions from readers, together with his own personal savings, would be used to cover the rest, namely airfare, insurance, a digital camera, bribe money (in cash), a gas mask and other protective gear, atropine ('for nerve agents, but if I have to pull it out, it likely won't do any good at that point'), payments for translators, the hiring of drivers, and so forth. His initial estimate, based on a previous trip to the region, was that $8,000 to $10,000 would be sufficient for a six-week to two-month stay.

Allbritton described himself as being 'incredibly touched' by the 'outpouring of support' from those readers of Back to Iraq willing to contribute to the cost of making independent 'reportage with a voice' possible. Telling readers that they should be 'extremely proud' of themselves, he watched as the donations grew to $1,200 in the first five days alone. Expressing his gratitude, he stated the best thing to come out of the blog was:

> the realization that for the first time in my 13 years as a journalist, I'm able to practice journalism with only one responsibility – to the readers. No editors to impress, no advertisers to stroke, no colleagues to compete against. (Well, except for George over at Warblogging. Heh.) The support all of you have shown is tremendous, and I take the responsibility to provide you with news, commentary and context from the war and the following occupation very seriously. Again, thank you for supporting me in the my [sic] efforts to do that. (Back to Iraq, 22 February 2003)

No advertisements, he promised, would be appearing on the site. At the same time, he said that he would ensure that all donors were treated equally, regardless of the amount they contributed.

He was convinced that this involvement on the part of his readers would be shaping his reporting in ways that would improve its quality, while also offering a meaningful alternative to what other journalists were providing.

> I know it sounds presumptuous, but unlike the high-powered White House reporters, or the embedded correspondents with the troops, if the majority of my 800+ readers yesterday donated $5 each, you would have your own guy in the field with contacts among the Turks and the Kurds, people ready to help me get into the country and an eye on the ground when the shooting ends and the occupation begins.
>
> Look, I know I can't do much. I'm one guy. And I truly believe reporters from *The New York Times*, *The Washington Post* and other newspapers are doing their best in bad situations. But every story can benefit from having many sets of eyes looking at it, from a myriad of angles. The big guys will be able to get stories that I won't be able to, that's a fact of life. But with your help and support, I can report stories over in Iraq that the big guys can't or won't. It's not that I have a monopoly on truth or that they are hopelessly corrupt. It's just that the more people reporting on something the better. (Back to Iraq, 11 March 2003)

This conception of 'intrepid journalism' evidently resonated with users as the volume of contributions grew. It similarly attracted the attention of commentators alert to what was happening in the blogosphere, with favourable reports about Allbritton's efforts appearing in a wide array of news sites and publications.

Journalism that 'owes its sole allegiance to the readers', Allbritton was convinced, would offer a significant alternative to the 'propaganda ploy' which embedded reporting in Iraq represented. 'While I may be the guy in the field, it's you, the readers, donors and supporters, who are building a new, new journalism (apologies to Tom Wolfe) through your patronage and readership', he declared. Credibility, he added, would be derived from 'the trust of the readers and a bubbling, robust and independent medium will be the result, as professional as anything that came before it, if not more so' (Back to Iraq, 15 March 2003). Part of this commitment to trust meant being up front about personal beliefs, in his view, not least with regard to the waging of the Iraq War itself. In pointing out to his readers that he claimed only to be independent, not unbiased, he proceeded to outline his opposition to the war. 'I think this war is the wrong war at the wrong time. One of the things that this web site allows me to do is to call bullshit when I think I see it' (ibid., 18 March 2003).

It was arguably this candid perspective that helped to attract users in increasing numbers to his blog. Bandwidth issues were becoming a problem by 19 March, by which time the server was being 'absolutely swamped' by more than 14,000 unique visitors a day. The sum of $10,000 was reached five days later, with every sign that the number of donors – over 300 by this point – would continue to grow. While busy with last-minute preparations, Allbritton paused to outline an additional part of his rationale for pursuing this approach to war reporting. Conceding that he was 'probably crazy', he insisted that he was hoping that the project would help to gain 'respect for the Web (and blogs) as a serious medium' for independent journalism.

Describing precisely where he was coming from was evidently one of the most compelling features of Allbritton's posts from Iraq once he was under way. In addition to sharing what he was discovering, combining first-person reportage with interpretive assessment of its significance, he took the time to respond to queries from his readers. Examples include:

What was the problem with the Iridium satellite phone?
There was nothing wrong with the actual phone, as it turns out. But for some reason I couldn't connect to the Iridium network that allowed me access to the Net. No connection, no email. And that was bad. This wasn't Iridium's fault, of course, but really more a connection issue between the Toughbook and the phone. Anyway, the data guys at Iridium set me up with a static IP address rather than DHCP and it's working fine now.

Why'd you use a dumb – and offensive – metaphor about the Bataan death march?
Because I was in such a hurry to get to sleep that I got lazy and used an inappropriate metaphor, for which I apologize,

especially to people who lost relatives in Bataan. What I experienced was not a death march. However, it was a forced march in that once I signed on, there was no stopping. I was physically hauled to my feet several times or pushed forward when I thought I was too far gone to continue. We climbed five or six mountains in pitch blackness, sometimes going high enough to trudge through calf-high snow. I hallucinated and became delirious. There was little water to drink and not much food. The language barrier was beyond frustration. Death march? No. But I honestly wanted to die several times.

When are you going to start reporting?
What, interviewing Kurds about their aspirations for nationhood isn't good enough? Talking with peshmerga about their support for the war too mundane? Should I be throwing myself into the pitch of battle immediately after a 36-hour forced march (see above)? I just got here. I left a little over a week ago, and I think there's been some decent reporting already. It's not Associated Press inverted pyramid-style writing, but I didn't think people wanted that on a site such as this. My reporting combines the personal, the micro and the macro. It's not necessarily new, but it works for me. (Back to Iraq, 5 April 2003)

As his blog's daily readership grew to upwards of 25,000, Allbritton became accustomed to receiving e-mails which posed questions and suggested story leads, while others provided useful links to online materials. 'My reporting created a connection between the readers and me', he later observed, 'and they trusted me to bring them an unfettered view of what I was seeing and hearing' (Allbritton, 2003). This involvement on the part of his readers (an example of the 'corrective power' of the medium's interactivity, to use his phrase) in shaping his reporting worked to considerable advantage – not least by helping to keep him honest about what he was seeing, and what it meant.

Allbritton was not alone in working as an independent blogging journalist from the conflict zone. While numbers are hard to establish, in 2003 there were at least half a dozen high-profile English-language 'sojo' blogs, as they came to be known. Their motivations were various. Some shared Allbritton's enthusiasm for the notions of greater independence of viewpoint and a closer relationship with readers. Others emphasized the less restricted authorial persona possible in the diary form, which they saw as allowing them to produce a journalism that could cross social and cultural boundaries more easily than reporters restricted by deadlines, the journalist pack and parochial news values.

Freelancer Joshua Kucera hoped that his blog, The other side (www.serendipit-e.com/otherside), would allow him to communicate something of the experience of being in Kurdish northern Iraq. In explaining the blog's title in his first post, he wrote:

> You can get good information from the New York Times, BBC and Associated Press. But you won't hear unvarnished opinion from a guy on the ground, or what ordinary days are like for the people here: about pornographic movie theaters, tragic love stories or the sunset over Erbil.
>
> Secondly, 'the other side' refers to the land outside America's borders, a big place that most Americans, even well educated ones, are not very familiar with. Reading the news about the Middle East or Indonesia or Venezuela is as about as meaningful as watching a game of Risk if you don't know what the streets smell like there or what people eat. I hope this blog can be a small substitute for that sort of experience. (The other side, 9 March 2003)

Kucera told a colleague he was 'blown away' by the relationship established with readers of his blog. His 'blog audience cared about him, worried about him, gave his work constant dialogue and feedback', a relationship which was not formed with the hundreds of thousands of readers of his writing in newspapers or magazines (Boese, 2004). His blog, however, did not last long, snagged by precisely the constraints on independence which Allbritton set up his site to escape. After a *Boston Globe* article suggested Kucera's blog entries were more immediate than the articles he wrote on contract for *Time* magazine, the magazine demanded he stop writing. Other journalists set up blogs for friends and family, where they recorded observations and accounts of their reporting work, and were surprised by the wider readership they attracted.

While some news organizations initially sought to shut down blogging by their staff, others experimented with the diary format's emphasis on what the individual journalist was seeing, feeling and thinking. Among these were *The Guardian*, whose reporter Audrey Gillan blogged on her experiences as an embed in the invasion phase with the Household Cavalry, and NBC, which encouraged a number of group blogs. Once the invasion became occupation, the network's Baghdad-based staff contributed to a blog titled Blogging Baghdad: The Untold Story. Blogging Baghdad was typical in aiming, as its 'about' page put it, to 'provide a dynamic look at the story behind the story of covering the news in Iraq'. The blog augmented the professional news product with a glimpse 'behind the scenes', relating the experiences of reporters and their reflections on their work. In particular, such writing emphasized a personal response to the political situation. NBC correspondent Becky Diamond wrote of her feelings after driving away from a bomb blast in Baghdad which nearly killed her, without pausing to help others caught up in it:

> The poor souls who were driving in an open pickup truck next to us had been bleeding on the ground while we were able to inch our way out. Stepping out of the car to help them was never an option – it would be suicide for westerners to get out of the car at that point. I hated myself for that and hated what Baghdad has become. (Blogging Baghdad, 5 May 2005)

This personal cry of anger and frustration, not appropriate in a tightly constrained television news piece, spoke volumes about the state of the country. As with Salam's or Allbritton's blogs, the intimate first-person narrative produced here invited readers to understand from Diamond's own individual perspective. Similarly, Steven Vincent, an independent blogger-journalist who won awards for his reporting from Basra at In the Red Zone (spencepublishing.typepad.com/in_the_red_zone) and who was killed after one of his exposés, wrote in a style which did not separate out his response to Iraq from his observations. Indeed, Vincent, a New York art critic, had gone to Iraq, and returned twice, because of a personal urge to understand the Middle East after being deeply shocked by the attack on the World Trade Center. On a number of occasions, he wrote angrily about the sexist treatment by Iraqi men of his 'fixer', a young woman journalist whom he called Layla in the blog. The individual performing the job of journalist was often well to the fore in such blogs, and the form appeared to be sought out by journalists who perceived an impartial account as insufficient to tell the story of the war.

As a consequence, these diary-like accounts did more than just supplement the news. They differed in the way they made sense of events, being more personal, more subjective in style and also more grounded in a particular moment and place. Fox News Baghdad correspondent Steve Harrigan wrote, for example, of his incomprehension when seeing a televised video of the beheading of a Korean civilian associated with the US forces:

> When the pictures came up we crowded around the screen to see them, then people walked away and the mood in the room changed. Something was sucked out . . . I've seen three beheadings now but it does not get any more comprehensible even though the video, the gestures, the orange jumpsuits are the same in each of them, which worries me. How can you defeat an enemy if you cannot understand him? Those men standing there behind the Korean – where they come from, how they think, how they got there – I don't see it. It is beyond my experience. (Foxnews.com, 22 June 2004)

In a context of news management and commercial pressure, this situatedness was a strength not just in providing vivid accounts with which readers could personally engage but in building the credibility of those accounts. Harrigan communicates the extreme discomfort and disgust of someone too close to the violence in these raw, syntactically incomplete sentences. In doing so, much is revealed about what war does to those who live through it. Lyke, cited above, communicates the journalist's frustration of being in a war zone but seeing little of it aboard an aircraft carrier, and in doing so both steps outside the journalistic constraint of being required to produce news items even when there is little worth reporting and lifts the veil on the news management constraining her work. Rebecca MacKinnon, who ran a blog on North Korea from 2003 to 2004, blogged at length about her failure to get a visa to visit the country, reproducing an official letter accusing her of contributing to Washington's 'jungle of lies'. She reflected later that writing about the process of newsgathering under oppressive conditions not only contributed to her relationship with her readers but in itself 'provided insight into the nature of the regime' (MacKinnon, 2004).

All these journalists' reports emphasize the individual as she or he is performing as a reporter, and therefore provide meaning on a number of levels at once. In information theory's terms, the 'provenance' of the information as the view of one individual in a particular location and moment is available for all to see, allowing people to assess it better as knowledge (Rogerson, 2007). A number of journalist bloggers from the war zone noted that this less coherent, more immediate style of writing appealed to those who read them. Stuart Hughes, a BBC producer, kept an informal blog, Beyond Northern Iraq (stuarthughes.blogspot.com), in the early days of the war. Intended largely for family and friends, it quickly gained a much wider readership. Hughes observed that his style of writing, 'literally what came into my head, this is what I've been doing, this is whom I've spoken to', was seen by readers as more trustworthy than the more considered, polished work of BBC news (cited in Matheson and Allan, 2007). Allbritton similarly noticed 'the personal connection that can be established through the interactivity of the medium' (Allbritton, 2003: 84). 'Throughout it all', he wrote after he returned from Iraq, 'I maintained a personal tone in my writing as I tried to let people know what it felt like to be working and surviving during such an extraordinary event' (ibid.). Thus a claim to reportorial integrity emerged, not from the expert authority of the professional news organization, but from the personal attributes and relationship with readers of the reporter.

In other words, it can be argued that these journalists' blog posts appealed as 'real' accounts precisely because they crossed the line between the public persona of the reporter and the individual filling that role, allowing readers to go more deeply behind the scenes to the life of the correspondent. Not all blogs were so raw in style or so personal, but even those edited by newsrooms, such as the BBC's Reporters' Log, sought a more casual mode of address in order to capture something of the ephemerality of journalistic experience. There has been a growing recognition among news organizations of the advantages to be gained by encouraging more interactive forms of engagement with their audiences. The potential of blogs to help forge new relationships is especially valued where building trust is concerned. As suggested by one e-mail Allbritton received from a reader, trust in the blogging journalist's account depends upon a sense of a personal relationship with the reporter. Vital here is as much the confidence that the blogger is independent from editors or other managers as it is a question of style, where the unapologetically subjective, immediate and intimate approach of this situated journalism matters. Allbritton's reader wrote: '[I liked] the independence it gave you the reporter. No agendas except your own, which is perfectly acceptable to me. No one is totally objective, but you gave more personal perspectives of "behind the scenes" of what it takes to do what you do, which was terribly fascinating to me' (ibid.: 83). To such readers, the 'editorial, journalistic gauze', which muffles even the most dramatic live piece to camera, is removed in the blog.

This reliance on the individual reporter on the ground in Iraq was objected to by a number of journalists, however, precisely because it bypasses the disciplines of verification which traditionally underpin journalism's reality claims. *Christian Science Monitor* columnist Tom Regan, for example, argued that 'bloggers promise a more immediate experience of the news, one in which accuracy isn't regarded as being the most important element' (2003: 69). Steven Levy of *Newsweek* maintained that the 'reality of the moment' provided in the warblog was similar to that offered by live reports from embedded correspondents and subject to similar criticism. Both are 'shaped by the personal experience of the creator rather than gathering news from after-the-fact interviewing and document collection. They are delivered in the first person, creating a connection with the viewer that sometimes bulldozes over the deeper realities of the events' (Levy, 2003). We would emphasize, though, that there is an important difference between the television reporter's performance of live-ness and the journalist blogger's performance of selfhood. In addition, the televisual claim to show the real was quickly eroded, while the blog's claim of authenticity to experience grew as the ostensibly heroic war of liberation became an occupation with weakening legitimacy. In that context, the different kind of inde-pendence of the 'sojo' blogger to that of the embedded reporter, in particular the much lesser degree of dependence on military and media institutions, became readily apparent. This was, as Allbritton (2003) noted, 'journalism without a net on the Net'.

Total audiences for blogs have been relatively small through-out the Iraq conflict – a Pew Internet and American Life survey found only 4 per cent of US internet users read them in the war's initial stage (Rainie et al., 2003: 5). Still, more personal modes of communication, including blogs but also initiatives such as the provision of space on the Belo Media Group website (belointeractive.com) for journalists, US soldiers and families to post messages for each other (Sylvester and Huffman, 2005: 86), soon rose to a position of significance out of proportion to their size. One moment from 2004 encapsulates this point. As she was preparing to leave Baghdad in October that year for a period of leave, *Wall Street Journal* reporter Farnaz Fassihi sent a private e-mail to a number of friends about the frustrations of attempt-ing to report from a city descending into civil war. She wrote:

> I avoid going to people's homes and never walk in the streets. I can't go grocery shopping any more, can't eat in restaurants, can't strike a conversation with strangers, can't look for sto-ries, can't drive in anything but a fully armored car, can't go to scenes of breaking news stories, can't be stuck in traffic, can't speak English outside, can't take a road trip, can't say I'm an

American, can't linger at checkpoints, can't be curious about what people are saying, doing, feeling. And can't and can't. (Cited in Garfield, 2006)

Fassihi's outburst of frustration and fear – in a context where the US government was downplaying the worsening security situation – was rapidly passed from person to person in US media and political circles. It soon became the subject of news comment, some of it shocked at conditions she experienced in Iraq, some of it denouncing her for voicing a sentiment so clearly contradictory to official statements. For what her e-mail appears to have achieved was to make sense, with the authority of genuine emotion and first-person observation, of what had previously been merely, as one commentator described them, 'numbing' daily news reports of the killing of unknown people (Zremski, 2004). Fassihi expressed exasperation that this personal e-mail should make more of an impact on people than her carefully produced news reports: 'It still gets to me that people say, "It's that bad in Iraq? We had no idea." And I'm like, "What do you mean, you had no idea? . . . Have you been reading my stories?"' (cited in CJR, 2006: 66). But, as Reese Schonfeld, CNN's founding president, wrote in reply to Fassihi:

> To Fassihi's questions, I answer, Yes, I've been reading your stories, but 'I had no idea.' The detail of your first-person piece forced a recognition on me that was never conveyed by the conventional journalism printed in The Wall Street Journal. From the details I generalized and now look at the war through different eyes. (Schonfeld, 2007)

Like the blog, the personal-e-mail-made-public helps to explain why some found the traditional news account to be wanting. Subjective war journalism has a long history, of course, featuring names such as George Orwell and Ryszard Kapuściński, who succeeded in communicating much more than the facts of a given situation by employing narrative techniques to share how it felt. What characterized Fassihi's e-mail, though, was the way private reflections on the conflict became public property. Not only were readers given insights into the individual's experiences of war, but the accounts gained a high truth value through a perceived authenticity to experience. The quickly written personal e-mail, which for Fassihi herself fell well short of the criteria of news journalism, was 'real' because it was not a pre-meditated intervention in politics, and because it drew readers within a particular moment in the writer's personal narrative.

It is possible to point to a number of wider factors which facilitated this way of making sense. By late 2004, the failure of the US to bring peace and democratic government to Iraq, the growing evidence of atrocities being committed by US troops, the horrendous price being paid in human lives, and the recognition that mainstream journalism – as acknowledged by some of its most senior figures – had taken at face value the case for invading the country in the first place, all appeared to be factors in the gradual unravelling of the Bush (and Blair) administration's rhetoric. At the same time, frustration appeared to be building – certainly in the blogosphere, and from virtually all political perspectives – that too little was known about what was actually transpiring on the ground in Iraq. For what were largely practical safety reasons, it was no longer possible for Western reporters to work in most parts of the country. Stepping into the journalistic void were several individuals, such as documentary-makers Brian Conley and Steve Wyshywaniuk. They abandoned their plans to document what was happening in Iraq, choosing instead to hand over their cameras to Iraqi colleagues, asking them to prepare short documentaries of everyday life in Baghdad. Under the title 'Alive in Baghdad', these local journalists produced videos for the web featuring ordinary Iraqis' views, some of which were quickly picked up, through the site, by major news outlets, such as the BBC's 'Newsnight'. Against a context of Western broadcasters' inability to communicate how Iraqis understood the occupation and the intermittent civil war in their country, Conley made a similar claim for these personally oriented videos to that made for Salam Pax's blog and Fassihi's e-mail: 'this type of reporting, bringing firsthand stories from the people who experienced them . . . may soon become what is considered the highest form of journalism' (cited in Shen, 2006).

To round out this chapter's discussion, it is worth reaffirming that the two US-led wars in Afghanistan and Iraq witnessed the use of new communications technologies enabling journalists to send back reports from almost any location with relative ease. As with previous technologies, from the invention of shorthand to the lightweight video camera, journalists embraced the promise of the videophone, the laptop and the digital camera to offer better access to the real. On the one hand, new media allowed these wars to be reported with startling immediacy, providing vivid images of events and the people caught up in them. On the other hand, the technologies were used to bring reporters to the fore, the most intrepid of whom were revealed to be individuals willing to step beyond the support structures of news organizations in pursuit of the story. The news became contextualized – sometimes in terms of a military point of view, sometimes more in terms of the reporter's personal experiences – but all too rarely in terms of the experiences of the Iraqi and Afghani citizens themselves.

CHAPTER FOUR

The Citizen Journalist at War

Introduction

Contemporary war reporting, for all its many faults, is heir to a long tradition of individual reporters bearing witness to the brutality of war. Conscience, combined with writing skills and a willingness to confront violence rather than turn away, has characterized the reporting of the likes of J. A. MacGahan, who described atrocities committed by Turkish troops in Bulgaria in 1876, Martha Gellhorn, who recorded the civilian suffering of twentieth-century total war, and John Pilger, who compelled Western audiences to see the Cambodian genocide of the 1970s. The moral force of the carefully detailed description favoured by many of these writers is clear in one vignette from Gellhorn's account of Madrid during its siege in the Spanish Civil War:

> Women are standing in line, as they do all over Madrid, quiet women, dressed usually in black, with market baskets on their arms, waiting to buy food. A shell falls across the square. They turn their heads to look, and move a little closer to the house, but no one leaves her place in line. After all, they have been waiting there for three hours and the children expect food at home. (Gellhorn, 1998: 21)

As Zelizer (2007) points out, this kind of eyewitness reporting, which draws upon conventions of realism familiar from the novel, makes a powerful claim to tell the truth of war. To show through a closely observed account that 'I was there' serves to silence alternative versions from those who were not present at that moment or place and to align the viewer with the witness's stance. Technologies that record the event's images or sounds, particularly the television camera, have only increased the force of that claim.

This tradition is now in the process of change as news technology evolves apace. In recent conflicts, from Iraq to Sri Lanka, from Burma to Liberia, those mediating the ravages of combat are as likely to be non-journalists as to belong to Gellhorn's company of professional witnesses. Combatants, civilians caught up in the fighting, medical personnel, tourists, students, even mountain climbers, have provided some of the more compelling accounts and images of recent tragic events, raising major questions about the way conflict is represented and understood. Not surprisingly, however, the private individual – an 'accidental journalist' in the eyes of some – must cope with difficult choices without the benefit of the professional's experience, training or resources. What can be seen as a powerful advantage, namely a commitment to bearing witness – even if it means speaking truth to power – can prove to be extraordinarily difficult to sustain under pressure.

Consider an entry from the blog of a Palestinian mother and journalist, Laila El-Haddad, from 29 November 2006 (a-mother-from-gaza.blogspot.com). Under the title 'Humanity Lost', she describes the mundane misery of the Israeli economic blockade of Gaza. Palestinians, who had taken the opportunity of a rare opening of the border to visit the Egyptian town of Rafah, then waited for days to be allowed to cross back into Gaza:

> We stood and we waited and we cried and we returned back to Egypt yesterday, and again today. Us and thousands of others.
>
> It was anguish. Anguish and misery and desperation personified [sic] in every woman, man and child.
>
> One hour turned into two, then three, then five, as we stood shielding our eyes from the piercing midday sun on Wednesday, when we were told the Crossing would be opening for a few hours.
>
> Some wailed in exhaustion, others fainted; still others cracked dry humor, trying to pass the time. We stood, thousands of us, packed together elbow to elbow like cattle, penned between steel barriers on one end, and the riot-geared Egyptian security guards on the perimeter, who were given orders not to allow

anyone through until they hear otherwise from the Israelis and
to respond with force if anyone dared. (Raising Yousuf and
Noor: Diary of a Palestinian Mother, 29 November 2006)

El-Haddad's account has the power of eyewitness testimony.
Like Gellhorn's reportage from Madrid, it allows the reader to
see the misery rather than hear of it. Yet, unlike the foreign correspondent, who purports to act as the eyes (and conscience) of
the distant audience, El-Haddad writes as both narrator and participant. She describes herself on the blog as a 'journalist, mom,
occupied Palestinian – all packed into one'. Her writing therefore
stands as eyewitness reporting, but of a particular kind. As a citizen caught up in war, she is no bystander or professional tourist,
as the journalist, however committed, inevitably is. She cannot
walk away and therefore writes with a particular stake in the
suffering she recounts. The suffering is part of her identity, not
something she must strive to relate to in some abstract sense. To
a young Lebanese man, Mohammad Soubra, who posted videos
on YouTube of the July 2006 Israeli bombing of Beirut, this distinction is enormously important. Television journalists who
report to camera with scenes of destruction behind them, he told
a journalist, are 'reporting without passion' and without depth of
understanding of the impact of war: 'I want people to see another
impact of war. How you can't sleep at night because bombs are
going off outside. I wanted people to see this and debate it' (cited
in Garofoli, 2006). Underlying these actions is a claim, although
one usually left implicit, that what they see and record is more
true to the lived experience of war than news reporting – and that
it is ethically superior.

Moreover, in providing their personal versions of the experience of war, El-Haddad, Soubra and others are making more
difficult one of the bases upon which war is fought, the silenc-
ing of the humanity of the Other. Their writing, grounded in
their refusal to accept their status as mere pawns of war, draws
strength from the challenges rendered to journalism's status as
society's authoritative knower – not least, the tensions engendered by the ideal of impartiality – in order to assert the value

of the individual participant's account. Increasingly, we find the idea of independence used to cover independence both from 'big media' and from military or political authorities. In the words of one of Iraq's first bloggers, Salam Pax, whose writing from Baghdad forged a complex identity that was reducible to neither Western nor anti-Western sentiment: 'Please stop sending emails asking if I were for real, don't believe it? then don't read it. I am not anybody's propaganda ploy, well except my own' (Where is Raed?, 21 March 2003). His blog entries radically disrupted boundaries of both a political and cultural nature (as indeed did El-Haddad's blog, which crossed barriers at which her body was literally stopped). In doing so such voices do not, however, step outside either politics or war. Indeed, the notion of 'new wars' discussed earlier suggests that these voices can be as easily read as participating in emerging forms of conflict as stepping outside them. If the 'virtuous war' discourse described by Der Derian (2001) exploits technology in order to tidy up war, to represent it as humanitarian, clean and distant when viewed from the perspective of those firing the missiles or dropping the bombs, here actors use technology to disrupt that discourse. The ostensible reasonableness of Israeli actions in restricting movements, as seen from the West, appears inhumane and vindictive from the perspective of the queue at the border crossing, even echoing the cattle wagons of the Holocaust or Shoa.

As Kaldor (2003, 2006) reminds us, contemporary wars are difficult to see in terms that separate military engagements and civilian populations. The citizen is not a bystander but central to the logic of conflict in which fear and insecurity are tools in the mobilization of people for political ends. Civilians are targets of human rights abuses, spectacular targets to terrorize others, potential citizen soldiers in ideological war. In this context, one could expect to see individualized digital technologies, such as the cell phone or personal computer, become tools deployed in that war. As this chapter suggests, the mediascape of conflict is increasingly one in which individuals are participating in both the media and the conflict through their self-representations.

We explore first the way citizen accounts of war have intersected with news media, considering news organizations' tentative steps towards using citizen witnesses in their reporting and the implications this has had for the representation of war. Next, we examine the alternative networks of information which have emerged alongside the news media, a phenomenon which raises questions around the ability of states to monitor or control the mediation of war. We then conclude with an assessment of the state response to these media, particularly the tendency to draw citizen-produced media into propaganda work.

The rise of citizen journalism

Since the beginnings of newspaper journalism in the seventeenth century, individuals have corresponded with editors about battles or other violent political events they observed or participated in. Right up to the start of the twentieth century, a figure such as Winston Churchill was able to move between the roles of soldier and correspondent as he fought in the British military campaign in Sudan in 1898. Indeed, the armchair generals who were so prominent in the US news media during the invasion of Iraq recall, if faintly, that tradition. What makes the rise of digitally mediated accounts of war by non-journalists in the early years of the twenty-first century so distinctive, however, is the way they can actively rewrite the more traditional relations of communicative power.

The power of the London *Morning Post* to reject Churchill's commentary was much greater than the power of today's editors to ignore the myriad voices now being heard from war zones in blogs, content-sharing sites and other digital media. This is partly a practical matter of the internet and cell-phone networks enabling text and images to be distributed from even the most far-flung war zone with near instantaneity, without the need for the specialist equipment and support intrinsic to a news organization's operation. It is also partly a matter of what Jenkins (2006) terms 'read–write culture' – the increasingly common practice of individuals producing media for the benefit of virtual communities, only sometimes electing to share these with more distant publics. Little of this self-mediated material, facilitated by social networking software such as Blogger.com, Facebook, MySpace, YouTube, Flickr or Twitter, overlaps with what has been characterized in the past as war reporting, but, when dramatic events happen, some of these web users suddenly find themselves at the scene of events (or, much more likely, intent on expressing their views on other people's news reports). This convergence of technological imperatives and cultural identities has weakened the boundaries which journalism has typically helped to reinforce between public news and private views. Ethan Zuckerman, one of the founders of Global Voices (an online hub for international bloggers), describes the voices of activists, citizens, non-governmental workers and soldiers in these personal media as 'a fascinating backdoor' opening up on global political affairs (cited in Norton, 2005).

Since the early years of the new millennium there has been a steady increase in the amount of citizen journalism – or user-generated content, as it is sometimes called – available across the webscape. The Al Qaeda attack on the World Trade Center's towers on 11 September 2001 proved to be a key moment when its reportorial value for public debate began to take shape. Blogs, discussion boards, personal homepages, and the like were transformed within hours into important resources for New Yorkers and others seeking more detailed information about the events – and the fate of people they knew. While television led the coverage, particularly with the spellbinding, shocking images of the towers and the Pentagon, web users' first-hand postings contributed a more personalized dimension to the imagery, often poignantly so. While major online news producers struggled to cope – their servers so overwhelmed by the sheer volume of users that pages were unable to load – this alternative network of sites stepped into the breach. For example, staff at Scripting.com, a site usually devoted to discussions of web programming, redistributed news items from those hard-to-access news sites and also posted eyewitness accounts and photographs. One of the site's writers later commented on the success of this accidental experiment in 'citizen journalism':

> The Web has a lot more people to cover a story. We, collectively, got on it very quickly once it was clear that the news sites were choked with flow and didn't have very much info . . . There's power in the new communication and development medium we're mastering. Far from being dead, the Web is just getting started. (Cited in Kahney, 2001)

Wired.com news editor Leander Kahney later remarked that the 'news coverage thus far has been heavily skewed to talking heads, while the Internet has overflowed with (talkative) New Yorkers and DCites, telling the real story.' It quickly became a common observation among journalism commentators that the status of the internet as a news source in its own right had been dramatically recast, thanks to the range and diversity of contributions provided by ordinary citizens caught up in extraordinary circumstances. Much the same has been said – indeed the echoes are striking – in relation to US soldiers blogging about their experiences from Iraq in 2003, holidaymakers' images of the tragic aftermath of the South Asian tsunami (when the phrase 'citizen journalism' entered the journalistic lexicon), or the sharing of information online by Wenchuan residents after the 2008 earthquake, among a plethora of other examples (see Allan and Thorsen, 2009).

Nevertheless, what is often characterized as the 'gatekeeping' role of journalism's established institutions remained largely intact in the aftermath of September 11 (see also Zelizer and Allan, 2002). The very limited news space given to critical assessments of US foreign policy, for example, let alone to voices of dissent from the non-Western world, underscored how the normative boundaries of 'debate' were being policed in ideological terms. In according legitimacy to certain views at the expense of alternative ones, the dynamics of media power set in motion a consensual frame whereby inconvenient facts or opinions could be safely ignored, trivialized or effectively silenced altogether (as Hallin (1986: 54) noted with regard to the reporting of the Vietnam War, there are certain 'political actors and views which journalists and the political mainstream reject as unworthy of being heard'). Still, to the surprise of some, it was becoming increasingly apparent that the mainstream news media were losing vital ground to these citizen media. Internet use soared as individuals went online to tell their stories, share their images, or offer up distinctive modes of understanding the events and their significance. Frustrated by mainstream reportage, many others actively sought out alternative sources of news, information and comment from across the web, often finding themselves in unfamiliar territory where US perspectives were more often than not openly challenged.

Similarly, while television stood accused of fetishizing live images of the bombing of Baghdad, bloggers on the ground with first-hand experience of the destruction and resulting human misery were drawing audiences into their realities through the vividness of their voices and their apparent independence from officialdom. The power of such accounts to disrupt the journalistic claim to provide privileged access to the reality of the conflict was considerable. Seasoned news professionals, while recognizing citizen media posed a challenge to their authority, nevertheless accorded them credibility when it seemed appropriate. The status of Salam Pax, for example, as an authentic voice of everyday life in Iraq as the US prepared to invade was to a significant extent created in media institutions both on- and offline. Salam became something of a celebrity, as *New York Times* writer Peter Maass noted in the online magazine Slate.com:

> The vitality and fearlessness of Salam Pax's writing, as well as the mystery of who he was – Iraqi? CIA? Mukhabarat? Jayson Blair? – led to stories by CNN, the New Yorker, and the Village Voice, among others, as well as a virtual felled forest of postings on war blogs and other sites: Instapundit mentioned him on two dozen occasions. Salam Pax was the Anne Frank of the war – I borrow that phrase from Nick Denton – and its Elvis. (Maass, 2003)

Zuckerman (2008) notes the irony that citizen media gain much of their public profile from the attention paid to them by the institutions they set out to challenge. When the Tunisian government denied its citizens access to the French DailyMotion video-sharing site to prevent access to a video criticizing the use of the presidential jet by President Zine Al Abidine Ben Ali's wife to go shopping in Europe, many more Tunisians became aware of the scandal as a result. The scale of the response to citizen media by society's dominant institutions is one of the drivers of their growing influence on media and politics.

The bombings in London on 7 July 2005, evidently the work of a group linked to Al Qaeda, provides a marker of the extent to which Western news reporting of conflict has had to reorient itself to accommodate the self-mediation of citizens, particularly in relation to breaking-news coverage. Within minutes of the multiple bomb blasts on underground trains and a bus, the first of hundreds of people were uploading their own images or writing their own accounts of the events on their blogs or personal webpages, as well as on media-sharing sites and websites such as werenotscared.com (the latter intended to allow Londoners to express solidarity with each other). Included among these impressions, observations and opinions was often highly accurate, timely information about what was happening on the city streets (and beneath them) as the crisis unfolded. Linehan (2005) believed that 'the interlinked, constantly updating world of the web provided a faster, more detailed picture of what was happening on July 7th than could be gained by passively watching TV's rolling news coverage.' It soon became apparent that significant numbers of these witnesses regarded what they were doing as intersecting with journalism, as they sent in their material to mainstream media, particularly the public service broadcaster the BBC. Head of news Richard Sambrook later recalled: 'Within six hours we received 1,000 photographs, 20 pieces of video, 4,000 text messages and 20,000 emails' (Sambrook, 2005: 12). Indeed, there was disquiet expressed by some victims at passers-by who got in the way of rescue efforts and intruded on privacy in their enthusiasm to act as citizen reporters. One blogger, Justin of piff.co.uk, wrote that, as he emerged from a train station, 'people with cameraphones vied to try and take pictures of the worst victims. In crisis some people are cruel' (cited in Glaser, 2005). Here there is evidence to suggest that many citizens at such moments regard the line between 'the public interest' and 'what interests the public' to be easily crossable. In response to this wave of citizen reporting, and in recognition of its value as a kind of journalism, several news organizations began to integrate the material into their reports as news footage, and not as secondary or supporting material to the professional journalist's account. The BBC led its evening news bulletin the day after the bombings with footage taken by members of the public, individuals who were present either on underground trains or who arrived on the scene moments afterwards. Sambrook talked of a Rubicon having been crossed in the organization's understanding of its relationship with the audience: 'The quantity and quality of contributions moved them beyond novelty, tokenism or the exceptional, and raises major implications that we are still working through . . . From now on, news coverage is a partnership' (Sambrook, 2005: 12).

Other broadcasters have responded similarly at moments of violence or natural disaster, seeking ways to draw this burgeoning of citizen witness accounts within the news operation. By 2006, CNN set up a site called iReport to gather and present news images – and to a lesser extent text – from citizens, including images from the Israeli bombing of Lebanon in August 2006. In a similar way to journalists' blogs, discussed in the previous chapter, the immediacy of a personal, impassioned account from a citizen of Beirut or a hurriedly taken image on a cell phone from a bombed train is contributing to the renewal and rewriting of the tradition of witnessing by which war reporting has traditionally given itself ethical and epistemological credibility.

'Every assassination will have its Zapruder'

It was by extraordinary chance that the assassination of US President John F. Kennedy on 22 November 1963 was captured on an 8 mm home-movie camera by clothing manufacturer Abraham Zapruder. In stark contrast, it has become common in recent times for violent events, such as the shooting by Chinese border patrols of Tibetan pilgrims making their way across a high Himalayan pass to India in 2006, or the assassination of Pakistani politician Benazir Bhutto in 2007, or the killing of Japanese photojournalist Kenji Nagai by a Burmese soldier earlier that same year, to be videoed on hand-held digital cameras or cell phones by members of the public standing nearby.

On the face of it, this new phenomenon vastly broadens the scope for news organizations to provide images of conflict that hold the powerful to account. When Bhutto was assassinated in the Pakistani city of Rawalpindi, official claims that she had died after hitting her head on a sun-roof lever when a suicide bomber blew himself up near her vehicle were soon undercut by cell-phone images taken by individuals at the scene. These images, shown on Pakistani and British television, quickly gave credence to her supporters' claims that she had been shot by an individual who had breached the insufficient government security arranged for her. Naím (2007: 105) regards such material from citizens as radically extending journalism's democratic functions. He notes that even the largest news organizations 'will never be as omnipresent as millions of people carrying a cell phone that can record video'. Like the 'CNN effect' – the reputed power of images of abuses, famines and uprisings broadcast on international television to drive foreign policy – he envisages a 'YouTube effect' in which human rights abuses, in particular, will be less likely to take place on account of the prevalence of cameras. Linehan (2005) similarly imagines the way this technology could force a greater respect for human rights into warfare. Referring to the massacre of an estimated 8,000 men and boys in the Bosnian town of Srebrenica in July 1995, he asks: 'Could Srebrenica have happened in the age of the cameraphone? Probably. Could our governments have pleaded ignorance of it at the time? Probably not.'

Certainly the wide distribution of camera phones and video

cameras in many countries, together with growing access to the internet, is providing news organizations with an ever greater quantity of dramatic images and first-person accounts from distant war zones. This material possesses the potential, in principle at least, to propel certain issues onto the international political agenda. Still, beyond cases such as the London bombings, it remains a constant challenge for news organizations to ascertain its relative newsworthiness (having first confirmed its veracity). According to Pick and Good (2006), much of the time the material gathered by citizen reporters (as well as by stringers, for that matter) in Iraq during the US occupation was simply too graphic or ideologically challenging for Western news organizations to consider showing, particularly footage or testimony of the violence of US occupying forces. They cite a number of independent Iraqi journalists interviewed for a 2006 British Channel 4 documentary who claimed that their news reports were filtered, effectively censored by the media. Sontag (2003: 10) notes that images of dead children during the ideologically charged Bosnian conflict were used by both Croats and Serbs in media briefings, suggesting the impact of Linehan's hypothetical cell-phone video from Srebrenica would depend to an extent on its accompanying and competing interpretations. Indeed, some politically explosive images from Iraq have been argued over in this way. In January 2006, a video showing bodies being removed from homes in Haditha, in Iraq's Al Anbar province, was sent to Human Rights Watch, which passed it on to *Time* magazine, where a reporter used it as evidence of a likely massacre of twenty-four civilians by soldiers of the US Marines, allegedly in retribution for a road-side bomb which had killed one of their colleagues (McGirk, 2006). Critical bloggers quickly sought to poke holes in the evidence. Some questioned why the individual who passed on the video, Abdel Rahman Al Mashhadani, waited four months before doing so; others questioned the motivations and credibility of various witnesses; still others pointed out perceived differences between witness accounts (see Feldman, 2006). The doubt created by these bloggers about whether or not a massacre had occurred can only have reduced the public pressure for accountability, and indeed, by the end of 2008, cases against all but one soldier involved had been dropped.

Quite quickly, then, the citizen reporter who threatens vested interests within a particular society risks losing her or his status as a witness, possibly being defined instead as an individual with an agenda to advance or an axe to grind. A news organization, in turn, which may otherwise be inclined to make use of this citizen reportage, becomes vulnerable to similar lines of criticism. Al Mashhadani, mentioned above, had his credibility challenged because he had worked as an election monitor for an Iraqi political party (Feldman, 2006). The *Time* reporter, Tim McGirk, was attacked as a leftist, someone whose impartiality was suspect because on a previous assignment he had spent Thanksgiving with the Taliban only two months after the 9/11 attacks. These tensions help to explain why it was the better part of two years before the first Western news organization, *The Guardian*, treated Salam Pax as more than a news event and as a news source in his own right. Before that date, Salam's blog appears to have been frequently discussed, but almost never quoted as a source of news on events in Baghdad. Much of the time it appears that citizen media are not easily absorbed into existing news form or practice because of the absence of sufficient institutional authority behind them.

In addition to those occasions when citizen media provide incontrovertible evidence of atrocities, important contributions of a different nature are being made on a much more regular, even routine, basis in war zones. Individuals caught up in trying circumstances who are able to relay what is happening to them may find their accounts valued by news organizations as much for their subjectivity as for any ostensibly objective record of facts which can be gleaned from them. US soldiers' documentation of the invasion and occupation of Iraq, via laptops, cell phones and digital cameras, provides a good example. The author of Armor Geddon, US tank officer Neil Prakash, provided remarkable insights into his state of mind as a decorated soldier in his blog entries concerning the storming of Falluja in November 2004. Prakash neither apologized for, nor distanced himself from, what was an obvious pleasure in killing. Instead his blog – until it was closed down by US authorities – celebrated the assault as a triumph of US military technology, of comradeship and of simply being alive. The values of socially acceptable public discourse, including regard for others' lives and for the seriousness of what was happening in Falluja, were suspended. In the following excerpt, Prakash's teeth-brushing one morning is interrupted by sniper fire:

> 'Good lord. Where the hell is it coming from?' It was funny as hell as we all looked around bewildered. It's a funny thing about getting sniped. You're probably waiting for me to elaborate, but I can't. That's it. It's just funny. Ok . . . so some guy has you in his sights and he's trying to kill you. And he hasn't yet. But the bullets are coming damn close. And you don't know where he is. So that's funny. And for some reason, any time you come real close to death, but live . . . that's just absurdly funny. (Armor Geddon, 28 December 2004)

Very few journalists reported from within the city of Falluja, partly because it was so dangerous. Journalists were caught between insurgents, with a reputation for targeting those who did not subscribe to their ideology, and the overwhelming power of the US attack (Palmer and Fontan, 2007). It was therefore difficult to substantiate concerns raised by the likes of Kevin Sites (discussed in chapter 1) or by non-governmental organizations about breaches of human rights and 'just war principles' there – one journalist stated that, 'As far as journalism is concerned, the shutters have come down' (White, cited in Feuilherade, 2004). Milblogs such as Armor Geddon therefore hold particular importance for the window they provided on the storming of a still inhabited city by the US's largest military operation since the initial invasion of Iraq. However, while details in the blog bear out some humanitarian concerns, Prakash's emphasis is typical of many accounts by US soldiers in Iraq in remaining on the level of intense personal experience. It offers, then, 'unprecedented access to the day-to-day reality of war' (Agrell, 2005), while saying little about the larger picture. As the excerpt above suggests, Prakash rarely elaborates. His writing has less to do with the political or the journalistic realms than with taking the reader into the lifeworld of those tasked with carrying out a war-fighting strategy.

This is not to deny its value, of course. As another US soldier in Iraq, Danjel Bout, told an interviewer, the blog form, situated in the moment in which it is written, allows readers to see beyond the 'militainment' representations of war shared by popular culture and much news reporting:

> Americans are raised on a steady diet of action films and sound bites that slip from one supercharged scene to another, leaving out all the confusing decisions and subtle details where most people actually spend their lives. While that makes for a great story, it doesn't reveal anything of lasting value. For people to really understand our day-to-day experience here, they need more than the highlights reel. They need to see the world through our eyes for a few minutes. (Cited in Hockenberry, 2005)

There are many versions of citizen war reporting, but a feature they tend to share is some sense that the wider public should hear the experiences of those in the war zone – and that, concomitantly, the third-person witnessing of professional journalists fails to communicate that experience. This is apparent whether the author is Faiza Al Arji, a middle-class Iraqi mother using her blog to lambaste the prejudiced reporting of women in the Middle East by Fox News (Al Arji, 2006), or Mohammad Soubra, cited above, posting videos from Beirut residents that would give viewers some inkling of how it feels to live in the midst of bombing, or Bout, seeking to communicate something of more 'lasting value' by detailing the daily life of a soldier. Zuckerman of Global Voices suggests: 'I think what it really has to do with is being listened to' (cited in Norton, 2005). Implicit in that plea to be heard is also a claim that the perspective of an individual speaking outside the frameworks provided by society's dominant institutions has intrinsic value. A significant cultural shift, it seems, is under-pinning the wider citizen journalism movement. The citizen, the amateur, the individual, the passionately partisan and the victim caught up in events all become categories of value, associated with claims to authenticity, the authority of personal experience and independence.

The new network news

By themselves, blogs such as the ones described above do not pose a significant challenge either to journalism or to the mili-tary. More important is how the plethora of voices now available in digital media combines to form information networks which may, potentially, reorient the social distribution of power and control at certain moments. Castells (2000) suggests that indi-viduals situated within these networks are becoming more powerful themselves in economic, political and cultural terms. Technological developments are perceived to be unravelling tra-ditional hierarchies, reconfiguring the geopolitics of information. In particular, institutions, ranging from nation states to multina-tional corporations, became less central to an emerging 'network society'. In contrast, the 'networked individual', in Wellman et al.'s (2003) phrase, moves relatively freely across political spaces made less stable or unified by the flows of information circulating around them. Bennett (2003) concurs, suggesting that 'lifestyle politics', an almost consumerist emphasis upon personal fulfil-ment, becomes more significant in shaping people's sense of self than institutions with entrenched ideologies.

A case in point is the rapid rise to significance of the blog of a weekend soldier, Bruce Rolston, in Canada. In the early months of 2003, Rolston's blog, Flit (www.snappingturtle.net/flit), became an up-to-the-minute compendium of information about the looming war in Iraq, gleaned from news, military and political websites and accompanied by his own sharp analysis. Allemang described Flit, based as it was in Rolston's personal and politi-cal interests, as providing a level of detail and interpretation in which no mainstream journalist would be able to engage on such a regular basis. 'No newspaper editor or TV producer would ever allow Mr. Rolston's work near a general reader or viewer, for fear of taxing or boring them', he wrote. 'But war creates a need to know and the desire to share expertise, whether it's about daily life in Baghdad, antiwar poets in New York, or where the war is going on the banks of the Euphrates' (Allemang, 2003). Rather than provide news of interest to a general readership, Rolston posted according to his individual preferences. In so doing, he became what network theory would describe as a node around which others who shared his political orientation, or who felt an affinity with the sense of self projected there, clustered.

In assessing the impact of these 'nodes' on journalism, it is apparent that much depends upon the strength of the individual's motivation to create a virtual community of like-minded individuals. Issues of trust in the quality of information-gathering are paramount. So, by way of further example, John Sloboda defends the website he co-founded to track the human consequences of the US-led invasion of Iraq, Iraq Body Count (www.iraqbodycount.org), both in terms of its rigorous methodology in gleaning information on civilian deaths from media reports and in terms of the passion for truth exhibited by its volunteer contributors. When asked in a media interview to justify the rationale for a website produced by 'amateurs', he responded that he and his colleagues were amateur in the sense of 'someone who does something out of a deep personal motivation. In that sense, absolutely, we are amateurs, rather than apparatchiks in some large organisation being paid to do this who don't care about it. We care about it passionately and deeply' (cited in BBC, 2006). Mediating between contending claims about casualties becomes a personal act of conscience in the face of the US military's refusal to publish its own body counts. In Castells's (2000) terms, the site belongs to the realm of networked media, where the 'apparatchiks' of Sloboda's disdain, whose power comes from their positions in institutional hierarchies or professions, lose influence to individuals who take personal responsibility for their position as nodes in the vast flows of information enabled by current technology.

The impact of the internet on public knowledge is complex, with likely as many commentators alarmed by a perceived fragmentation of the 'public sphere' as there are those enthusiastic about the emergence of an array of multiple public spheres. Certainly an individual's choice between competing news sources becomes a telling characteristic of their personal identity (see also Papacharissi, 2002). A number of critics point to a subtle, but nonetheless substantial change in public knowledge as individuals endeavour to supplement the provision of national media systems with alternative sources of news and public debate. Thurman (2007), for example, points to the remarkable popularity of British news stories contesting the arguments for war in Iraq among US readers – 73 per cent of the hits on *The Independent*'s site in September 2004 were from the US, and in November 2004 one *Times* story ('Backing Bush has won you nothing, Chirac tells Britain') by itself represented 15 per cent of its web hits from the US (see also Seib, 2003: 632). While greater choice of media is in itself by no means a guarantor of richer public debate, it appears that a significant number of people in the US used the opportunity of the internet to extend their horizons beyond the narrowly framed national ones on offer in much of the domestic media during the early years of the war in Iraq. Again, it is useful to think in terms of network theory, where the emphasis is placed on how individuals take on a certain kind of power through the ways they augment existing forms of information on conflict with what they can produce and consume online.

In the Middle East, Beckerman (2007) argues that transnational public opinion has begun to emerge in the Arab blogosphere, challenging the tight ideological constraints of official pan-Arab, nationalist and anti-Israeli media discourse. He traces the expansion of this blogosphere first in Iraq during the US occupation and then in places such as Lebanon during the so-called Cedar Revolution after the 2005 assassination of Prime Minister Rafik

Hariri. A vibrant network, which he estimates to involve some 25,000 Arab bloggers (many of them people in their twenties blogging in English, where 'breathing becomes easier'), emerged in the space of two to three years. While competing perspectives on war and crisis reporting are available in some of the region's media, particularly among satellite television stations, blogs provide an invaluable space for individuals to voice opinions outside of the realm of accepted orthodoxies. As one Lebanese blogger, Abu Kais, observed:

> Every leader thinks they represent everyone in these countries. And I think that's something we challenge every day in our blogs. We challenge what they say, and we always show the politicians as hypocrites, really. We have documented what has happened over the past two years and are able to contrast statements that show the level of the hypocrisy. That's something you don't always find in Lebanese media. (Cited in Beckerman, 2007: 20)

Others point to the role of bloggers in Kuwait in 2006 in building a campaign for electoral reform – including the vote for women – a campaign which spilled onto the streets and led to concessions by the government. Beckerman emphasizes the power of these individualized blog networks to cross formerly impermeable boundaries in the Arab region between Christian, Muslim and Jewish communities. He cites one Israeli blogger, Lirun Rabinowitz, as typical. Informed by the personal perspectives of others, Rabinowitz railed against the ethnic demonization which so often emerges in times of conflict:

> You want to tell me that these people are stupid? Well, they're not. You want to tell me that these people want to live in a dictatorship? Well, they don't. You want to tell me that they can't be Muslim and tolerant and friendly at the same time? Well, it's wrong. You want to tell me that they hate me just because they're Muslim and I'm Jewish? Well that's wrong, too. And they prove that to me every day. And I get this amazing opportunity to dispel every demonic myth and every stupid stereotype that I could ever have thought of. (Cited in Beckerman, 2007: 23)

Although the Israeli war against Lebanon in 2006 hardened opinions on both sides, blogging across that divide not only continued but increased, with one blog site, lebanesebloggers. blogspot.com, receiving a quarter of a million hits during the month-long war. 'Lebanese and Israelis engaged each other at the deepest levels about the politics of the conflict, their fears, and sometimes even their hopes for the days after', Beckerman observed (ibid.: 21).

Still, it must be remembered that individualized networked media can militate against collaborative initiatives. Pickerill and Webster (2006) note that little in the way of political commitment to others is required of individuals who sign an online petition or post a comment on a discussion board. Lifestyle politics and the media which it produces are perhaps somewhat thin forms of civic participation, particularly when they collide with entrenched forms of power. Here the experience of the Syrian poet Ammar Abdulhamid is telling. He was able to cross from the literary to the political world by blogging his previously censored critical writings on Syrian current affairs. As he expresses it, his blog drew him further into politics, as he felt obliged to act on the beliefs he expressed there, leading to a peace dialogue emerging between Syrian and Israeli citizens. While freed to an extent from state control through his blog, Abdulhamid soon found himself exiled from his homeland. 'The internet is just an instrument and it cannot be divorced from the overall struggle for greater liberalisation of our system for greater freedom', he later reflected. 'We need to push our regimes' (Abdulhamid, 2006). The power of the individual to write her- or himself outside dominant institutions and into different structures of politics is evidently heavily constrained.

As virtual networks have gained prominence as sites of public debate, there are signs of news organizations making efforts to link them into traditional structures of news. For digital war reporting, this is by no means an easy process. It involves finding space for alternative forms of witnessing when ideological tensions make any form of journalism, let alone that produced by non-credentialed individuals, suspect in the eyes of critics. Hamilton and Jenner (2004) note, however, that new varieties of foreign reporters have begun emerging, sometimes driven by the quite pragmatic reasons that news organizations cannot afford to send staff reporters to certain areas, or because they are not prepared to take the required risks where their personal safety is concerned. One significant development in this regard has been the decision by Reuters, a global news agency, to include the contributions of bloggers as part of its news services. Since 2006, it has integrated news and commentary provided by an independent organization, Global Voices Online, which monitors hundreds of blogs from across the world, into, first, the AlertNet service it provides for non-governmental organizations and then, later, its Reuters Africa site. Global Voices' nine regional editors, based at Harvard Law School, link to blogs which they regard as providing good quality news and commentary. Moreover, they provide summaries and links to interesting blog entries, which Reuters also distributes. In a press release announcing the venture, Reuters stated that 'Global Voices feeds can provide the depth and context that traditional Western coverage, for whatever reasons, miss out on' (cited in Hogge, 2007). Its acknowledgement that the current Western news system underrepresents many countries, and that the subjective perspectives and knowledge of individual bloggers from those countries could add reportorial depth, signals a significant broadening of thinking. Reuters has long championed objectivity in its reporting, which makes this initiative especially interesting.

Networking media such as Global Voices have shown some success in giving greater prominence to a number of the world's otherwise less visible political and social conflicts (a problem directly tied to major news organizations' scaling back of resources, including correspondents posted in foreign places). In November 2006, Global Voices' Arabic editor/translator, Amira Al Hussaini, covered the outrage in the Egyptian blogosphere concerning 'an orgy of sexual harassment' against women in the streets of Cairo during the Eid festivities, which follow the abstinence of the month of Ramadan. Among the coverage were the (translated) words of one blogger, Malek:

> We saw a large number of men whistling and running in the direction of Adly Street. We went with them to see what was happening. I was surprised to see a girl in her early 20s falling on the ground and a mob of men gathering around her, feeling up her body and tearing her clothes off her. I didn't understand or rather I couldn't comprehend what was happening. The girl got up and ran into a restaurant and hid inside. (Malcolm X, cited in Al Hussaini, 2006)

Global Voices stated on its website that its report contributed to Western media scrutiny of the events, which increased pressure on the Egyptian government to respond. Similarly, the violent suppression of protests in Burma in September 2007 was brought to world attention partly through blogs interlinked by services such as Global Voices (*The Guardian*'s Newsblog was similarly prominent in making use of accounts provided by Burmese bloggers). Its East Asian editor Preetam Rai linked to (and translated) reports by individuals from within Burma, including first reports of violence such as the following:

> While they are trying to stop us, another military truck appeared from the Myanmar Archers Association Ward and shot gun fires. Some people were hit. I had to jump over the brick wall and ran into the school. I met other fellows who came and hid in the school. They said two people were shot while they were jumping over the wall. There were lots of gun fires either aiming at protestors or on the sky. During that time, the school wasn't over yet. There were parents who came and picked their children up. They even shot gunfires during that time. How bad were they! (Kaduang, cited in Rai, 2007)

Although Asian and Western media reported on the violence, the small number of locals with internet access, such as 'Kaduang', was without doubt an important source of initial reports of the government crackdown. Burma's military-led government, listed by Reporters sans frontières as among the world's worst in curtailing press freedoms (RSF, 2007), controlled the local media

Web-based networks allowed opposition groups within Burma to smuggle out images of violence very quickly during the protests of October 2007. Here, the body of Japanese photojournalist Kenji Nagai, shot at point-blank range by Burmese riot police as he was filming, is dragged from a Yangon street. © AFP/Getty Images

tightly and restricted access to international journalists during the political tensions. One observer, Thai-based US journalist Richard Ehrlich (2007), credits these citizen reporters with providing a window on events which would otherwise have been largely unseen by the rest of the world, as well as providing poignant insights into those individuals' attempts to continue to live their lives amidst the chaos. Some of the blogs he cites described their authors' personal fears, others what they had seen and heard, while yet others provided photographs with terse captions such as: 'now regime open fire into these group, and used fire engine to sweep the blood on the street.'

The immediate response of the Burmese authorities, to close down internet cafés and drastically restrict the volume of web traffic, making pictures and videos difficult to send, is testament to the political threat posed by individual citizens here. But nongovernmental organizations and networks, which ensured this material was more widely shared, were also vital. Ehrlich points to the role of websites produced by exiled Burmese journalists and other activists in amplifying the information coming out of Burma and interpreting its significance for the benefit of global media. These web-based 'bridging media', as Global Voices' founder, Ethan Zuckerman, describes them, are increasingly prominent, feeding material from near-forgotten areas of the world into the global news system. The Democratic Voice of Burma, based in Norway, was one route by which footage of the shooting by Burmese soldiers of Japanese photojournalist Kenji Nagai made its way out of the country and onto the international news agenda. It caused particular outrage in Japan, where the images evidently led to a hardening of the government's stance towards Burma.

The end of propaganda?

Many scholars, including Castells (2001), have argued that the emergence of new information networks is leading to a weakening of governmental authorities' influence over publics during times of national crisis. One aspect of this apparent weakening revolves around the extent to which official sources find themselves open to challenge, their very status as reliable, authoritative knowers being subjected to critique. When eyewitness bloggers from Burma or the amateur collation of casualties on Iraq Body Count begin to gain in credibility, the news media's dependence on official bureaucracies diminishes accordingly. 'Propaganda in the historical sense is simply not an option for contemporary governments', argues *The Guardian* reporter Owen Gibson (2003). He compares the Falklands/Malvinas conflict in 1982, where British journalists – and the public – were almost completely dependent on British officials for the transmission of news from the distant war zone, with the Middle East at the start of the twenty-first century. In the case of the latter, the sheer volume and diversity of competing accounts ensure that none can dominate the news agenda in any simple, straightforward way. Seib argues similarly that web-based independent media, such as Altmedia and Altmuslim, can 'dilute the potency of governments' "official news" which needs to face minimal challenge if it is to be effective' (2003: 630).

This argument, while on the optimistic end of the continuum, does find support in examples of the growing difficulties governments face in seeking to manage public opinion by controlling the news media. When the authoritarian regime in Kyrgyzstan began to crumble in 2005 and President Askar Akayev shut down opposition news outlets, the ability of opposition supporters to continue to report for a crucial further month via a blog site arguably contributed to the change of regime (see Sulikova and Perlmutter, 2007). In Thailand, a young blogger with knowledge of the finance industry, Sarinee Achavanuntakul, may have helped bring down Prime Minister Thaksin Shinawatra in 2006 by publicizing his business dealings, while others acted as critics of the military figures who overthrew him. Roasa (2008) argues that individuals such as these function as the only 'reasonably credible' sources of news in many countries where most media are state-controlled or of poor quality.

A further example is worth discussing in detail, as it illustrates the potential (if not the frequent realization of that potential) of information networks to resist the sharper excesses of media management. When the US government sought to escalate a military incident between three of its warships and Iranian patrol boats in the Straits of Hormuz at the entry to the Persian Gulf in early 2008, a number of bloggers and blog readers led major news providers in critiquing the official US account. Initially the *New York Times*, for example, reproduced the Pentagon version of the incident:

> Five armed Iranian speedboats approached three United States Navy warships in international waters in the strategic Strait of Hormuz on Sunday, then maneuvered aggressively as radio

threats were issued that the American ships would be blown up, military officials said Monday. (8 January 2008)

The Pentagon released a video of the speedboats, which it combined with an audio track of a radio message received by the ships at the same time: 'I am coming to you . . . You will explode after a few minutes.' Officials described the incident as 'reckless and dangerous' and, according to investigative historian Gareth Porter, phoned journalists to tell them that 'there was a near battle on the high seas' (Goodman, 2008). The Iranians countered that the incident had been a routine reconnaissance encounter in the tense waterway, denying that they had threatened the ships and releasing their own video with quite different audio to support their claim. They accused the US government of propaganda ahead of a visit by President Bush to the Middle East to build support for his bellicose stance towards Iran.

Within a day, the US version began to unravel in the face of critical analysis by non-official voices, some of them military experts with experience of this body of water. A former senior US Navy officer posted a comment on the *New York Times* Lede blog (thelede.blogs.nytimes.com) stating that, while the Iranian manoeuvres were aggressive, the US Navy would not have taken the radio warning seriously. The open ship-to-ship maritime channel was, he said, 'like a bad CB radio':

> Everybody and their brother is on it; chattering away; hurling racial slurs, usually involving Filipinos (lots of Filipinos work in the area); curses involving your mother; 1970's music broadcast in the wee hours . . . So my first thought was that the 'explode' comment might not have even come from one of the Iranian craft, but some loser monitoring the events at a shore facility. (Comment 152, The Lede, 8 January 2008)

Others, including Iranian-Americans, argued that the voice heard on the radio did not sound Iranian. A few days later, US counter-terrorism intelligence officer Malcolm Nance posted a long account of naval battles and tensions with Revolutionary Guard craft in the straits on the blog of an independent US military site, Small Wars Journal (Nance, 2008). He described the Iranian manoeuvres as 'serious but routine' for the area, and that the voice was probably not Iranian but from crew of a passing ship having fun at both sides' expense.

The White House and Pentagon soon backed away from their claims. Both the speed with which individuals writing online debunked them – particularly what appeared to be a dishonest splicing of audio into the video – and the extent to which professional journalists played catch-up are striking. Also noteworthy is the contrast with the 1964 Gulf of Tonkin incident. In 1964, the slowness of US military and political officials to correct initial, faulty reports that the North Vietnamese Navy had fired on a US ship – and indeed attempts to cover up the faulty use of intelligence in that incident lasted until 2005 – gave the Johnson administration a legal pretext to enter the Vietnam War (Shane, 2005). While the lack of enthusiasm within US political circles in 2008 for another war is a major factor in the deflation of Bush's anti-Iranian rhetoric, a much wider ring of critical voices also played a part.

Political persuasion is about much more than control of information, however. To a significant extent it is about control of frameworks of understanding. In this regard, news reporting in a liberal tradition, with its emphasis on balancing a range of competing perspectives in order to facilitate public debate, is perhaps less susceptible to control than some of the newer forms of mediation discussed above. One of the strongest criticisms of blogs, particularly in the US, has been that they act as echo chambers for fixed opinions among like-minded individuals, stifling rather than facilitating discussion. Keen's (2007) attack on the 'cult of the amateur' is typical of this critique. He describes the powerful networks of bloggers, particularly in that country, as radicalizing and fragmenting society. There is some statistical evidence to back up the point. A number of studies appear to show that the highly opinionated warblogs which emerged in the US and other Western countries in the wake of the September 11 attacks, for example, have operated to render communities of users more polarized and inward-looking, possibly leading to opinions becoming entrenched (see Wall, 2005).

Some of this (often vituperative) blogging, particularly on the political right, has focused on critiquing the 'liberal bias' of the news coverage provided by major news organizations – what some bloggers call 'fisking', after their favourite target, *The Independent*'s Middle East correspondent Robert Fisk. Since the early years of the US occupation of Iraq, these blogs have zeroed in on reports which, in their eyes, are overly negative in their appraisal of the state of the conflict. The influence of these blogs can be considerable at times. A roar of anger from bloggers concerning the *New York Times*'s decision not to report a march of 10,000 Iraqis against terrorism and for democratic government in December 2003 forced an admission from the newspaper's public editor to a leading blogger, Glenn Reynolds, that the paper's staff had 'dropped the ball' (see Au, 2004). In February 2005, CNN's chief news executive Eason Jordan resigned after a concerted campaign against him by bloggers, ignited by comments he made at a World Economic Forum meeting which suggested to some that he believed journalists were being deliberately killed by US troops in Iraq. (Eason and other journalists at the forum later said the point being made was about individual journalists deliberately shot by soldiers thinking they were insurgents; see Kurtz, 2005.) To some commentators, particularly other journalists shocked at the loss of a senior news executive over an unguarded remark, the campaign was a witch-hunt fuelled less by a desire for truth than to score points against a news network perceived as too liberal (see Allan, 2006; Rosen, 2005). Similar concerns were expressed when, in 2006, a network of bloggers sought to prove that an Iraqi photographer working for the Associated Press, Balil Hussein, was in fact working with insurgent groups. One blogger in particular, Michelle Malkin, who also worked as a columnist for various media, called the organization the 'Associated (with terrorists) Press' and cited intelligence sources who had been suspicious of Hussein's apparent ability to turn up at assassinations and car bombings within minutes (Malkin, 2007). Hussein spent two years in detention before being released after a review of evidence by Iraqi judges rejected all charges.

Media of the long war

Examples of this sort suggest that the term 'citizen war reporting' may be something of a misnomer for aspects of the mediation of conflict by individuals outside the news media. One of the trends apparent across the range of these instances concerns the blurring of categories such as journalist, combatant, official, citizen, activist and victim within a context of multiple, at times contradictory, inflections. While figures such as the Syrian poet Abdulhamid find themselves ostracized, others such as Malkin find themselves drawn closer to the state. Indeed, as is argued below, governments and non-state military actors can be seen to be taking advantage of such blurred lines not only in order to distribute propaganda, but also to colonize spaces such as blogs and discussion sites with a view to influencing public opinion.

Changing conceptions of war demand constant vigilance on the part of journalists and citizens alike. The growing 'weaponization of information' (Schulman, 2006), in the strategists' phrase, is especially significant in this regard. As discussed in the previous chapter, near real-time journalism may pose an intelligence threat to military dominance on the battlefield. On a wider level, the importance of media in public life means that the public's support for war must be fought for before the enemy is engaged. Indeed, theorists of war such as Gray argue that contemporary war is often a contestation of power more over information than it is over space. Subcommandante Marcos, the leader of the Zapatistas in the Mexican state of Chiapas, spoke of disrupting state power through publicity as much as violence: 'We did not go to war on January 1 [1994] to kill or to have them killed. We went to make ourselves heard' (cited in Gray, 1997:

6). War for them was a means of publicity and was supported by the use of e-mail and discussion groups (see also Russell, 2001). The new ideological war on 'terror' in which the Bush administration imagined itself during its terms of office (also called 'the long war') was in some ways similar. Like the Cold War binarism between East and West before it, this war has been fought over perceptions of national security rather than territory per se. 'When we refer to the long war', Pentagon policy official Ryan Henry told reporters in 2006, 'that is the war against terrorist extremism and the ideology that feeds it, and that is something that we see going on for decades' (cited in Tisdall et al., 2006). Groups arranging themselves against the West, or specifically against the US, sometimes speak in similar terms. Relevant here is Kaldor's (2003) conception of 'network war', where, on one side at least, non-state actors are organized less by national identity or formal institution than by shared politically extreme narratives (the internet, along with DVDs and audio tapes, becomes a central tool in these loose coalitions).

In many conflicts, where mainstream media are controlled by the state, combatants have turned to the micro-media of cell phones, blogs, discussion sites and media-sharing sites to further their aims and objectives. In occupied Iraq, where the US-aligned government has exercised control over many television stations and newspapers, some commentators regard the television station Al Zawraa as playing an important role in fomenting the Sunni uprising. The station, initially beamed in via the Nilesat network, showed short videos, many probably recorded on cell phones, of roadside bombs targeting US troops, rocket-propelled grenade attacks on US bases, and the like. In addition, the wide availability of the cell phone has allowed such videos to be both recorded and distributed among personal networks. BBC correspondent Andrew North (BBC News Online, 7 February 2005) credits this technology with giving 'the insurgents a ready made network to spread their message, and putting the Americans and the Iraqi Government on the back foot'. In a related example, the initial controversy among Muslim groups over cartoons of the Prophet Mohammed published in the Danish newspaper *Jyllands-Posten* was fanned by messages sent via cell phones. These messages included ones calling on people to attack embassies around the world, with one (falsely) announcing that copies of the Qur'an were being burnt in Copenhagen's central square. One Danish politician remarked at the time: 'These messages are now part of the conflict' (cited in Sullivan, 2006).

In a further example of how micro-media are being increasingly 'weaponized' as part of asymmetrical warfare, Klopfenstein (2006) argues that since 2001 there has been a corresponding change in what the West has termed 'terrorism'. Specifically, the use of violent acts against civilians in order to intimidate them has been made simpler now, he argues, because groups can amplify the violence themselves through media they control. Before the internet, non-state actors using violence as a form of publicity could not be sure that the television cameras would be there, or that the news coverage would mention their aims. Now, he observes, 'terrorists can take whatever message and images they decide to straight to the online world, and that world is global in reach' (2006: 106). The online distribution of brutal images of the execution of *Wall Street Journal* reporter Danny Pearl is widely cited as an example of this 'terrorist internet'. Of particular concern here is that news organizations were drifting into a form of competition with these dramatic, violent media. CNN International president Chris Cramer (2004) has referred to a kind of 'digital anarchy' in which the rush to be first with breaking news precipitated news organizations into reproducing 'terrorist videos' and so allowing them to set the news agenda. Just as news organizations risk being drawn into state-sanctioned spectacles of violence, such as the 'shock and awe' bombing of Baghdad, which was clearly planned with cameras in mind, they can become complicit in the anti-state spectacles of the beheadings of hostages or suicide bombings. With both, journalists are in danger of being manipulated by the perpetrators of violence by dint of news values, namely the preference for dramatic events, graphic images and immediacy.

Walsh and Barbara (2006), in contending that a wider range of alternative voices was audible during the 2003 invasion of Iraq than had been the case during other recent major wars, nevertheless insist that the internet, by and large, has simply 'broadened the techniques available to states to try to shape public opinion'. In their view little has changed: 'the process of seeking to control war coverage remains fundamentally the same.' There are certainly signs that spaces which have been widely characterized as citizen media, from blogs to discussion spaces to content-sharing sites, are being targeted in military and political media management campaigns in much the same way that professional journalism has been targeted in the past. Furthermore, there is cause for concern that the still evolving reportorial forms and practices indicative of online media work to the advantage of those seeking to manipulate them. When individual citizen journalists, for example, claim independence because of their distance from the news institution (rather than their distance from the state), and declare a type of discursive authority based on their political commitment, precise roles and alignments become difficult to discern.

Some critics, for example, have accused US blogger Bill Roggio, widely regarded as an expert in military intelligence, of receiving support and funding from groups linked to US covert intelligence. In September 2007, Roggio, a former US soldier, turned his long-running warblog into a grander enterprise called the Long War Journal. According to him, some soldiers in Iraq had already been reading his blog for its more accessible version of military intelligence (McLeary, 2008). This new online publication sought to elaborate further the blog's blend of news and intelligence by bringing together a small team of individuals to report on terrorism, counter-terrorism and the world's many small wars, and to do so with a commitment to detail that news organizations would not match. McLeary argues that Roggio 'picks up where the mainstream press leaves off, giving readers a simultaneously more specific and holistic understanding of the battlefield', and, in particular, an empathy for soldiers 'born of shared experience' (ibid.). Roggio has also been credited with providing his readers with information and analysis that was months ahead of the press, including foreseeing a softening of the relationship between the Pakistani government and the Taliban in the tribal provinces of North and South Waziristan.

Roggio is explicit about the ideological frame in which he works. Public Multimedia Inc. (PMI), the non-profit organization that he founded to fund the endeavour, states as its aim: 'Accurate reporting of The Long War is critical for the American citizenry and her allies to make choices in the important decisions that affect their lives' (PMI, 2007). Roggio also makes no secret of his continuing links to the military. He has been invited to visit Iraq as an independent embed with US troops on numerous occasions and he is also associated with the US Department of Defense Bloggers Roundtable (on which more below). Some critics, however – particularly the author of the Bush Out blog, writing under the name 'Gandhi' – have pointed to possible links between Roggio and US government covert intelligence operations. Although Roggio says he relies on donations from readers to cover the costs of his seven staff as well as the journalists he has employed on assignment (McLeary, 2008), Gandhi points to acknowledgement on the Long War Journal website of the support of one of the larger charities distributing aid in Iraq, Spirit of America (SoA). SoA was originally set up by the Cyber Century Forum, 'a group dedicated to spreading US influence worldwide, with a particular emphasis on covert cyber-intelligence measures' (Gandhi, 2005). Some of SoA's activities suggest it is involved in much more than aid. It has provided computers, internet connections and its own Arabic blog software to selected Iraqis – one can presume to Iraqis whose political views it is inclined to endorse. Elsewhere SoA appears to have clearly politicized aims in the online initiatives it backs. The radical magazine *Counterpunch* notes its support in 2005 for protestors against the pro-Syrian government in Lebanon, including both money and facilitating the setting up of a large number of citizen blogs. It labels

SoA part of the 'regime change industry' (Schuh, 2005). Also linked to SoA are two prominent English-language bloggers in Iraq, the Fadhil brothers, who run Iraq the Model. The organization flew them in 2004 to Washington, where they were feted by President Bush and other senior Republican politicians. According to a third Fadhil, who acrimoniously parted company with his brothers, SoA also provided the bloggers with $300,000, presumably in payment for their pro-US blogging (Gandhi, 2007). Another blogger, on the basis of parallels in phrasing, accused the brothers of publishing under their name propaganda material written in the US State Department's 'public diplomacy' office (JuliaAnn, 2007).

Accusations such as these are hard to prove. There are many hundreds of websites promoting the US's policy in the Middle East, by soldiers in Iraq and their supporters, individuals of various political persuasions and a range of political groups. Other channels of citizen media, such as CNN's iReport, have also been targeted by individuals seeking to press the case against what they perceive to be the shortcomings of the 'liberal media'. It is immensely difficult to discern which of these instances simply involve passionate citizens, and which form part of a larger, institutionally orchestrated propaganda effort. The iReport contributor IQATF, for example, 'a retired special operations guy working as a contractor in Iraq', writes frequently and in glowing terms of the healthy state of the Iraqi police and military forces and their successes. To what extent is he indeed an independent, albeit enthusiastically supportive, commentator on the US's aims in Iraq?

What is clearer is that governments are aware of the advantages to be gained in using citizen media to further their military and political aims, especially where they can cloak such efforts in the mantle of independent media. Some parts of this activity are relatively open. The US State Department, for example, began employing Arabic- and English-language bloggers as part of its Digital Outreach Team in 2006. The *New York Times* reported that in their first nine months two Arab staff had posted comments on seventy websites, with the aim of reaching 'the silent majority of Muslims who might sympathize with Al Qaeda yet be open to information about US government policy and American values' (McFarquhar, 2007). It planned – and we can assume the plans were carried out – to employ a further seven bloggers to contribute in Arabic, Farsi and Urdu blogs and discussion sites. All were working on the basis that they had openly declared their affiliation when blogging, yet presumably with the hope that their more casual style would have greater impact than officials saying the same things. The blog comments were, in the words of the newspaper report:

> carefully written in English by the blogging team and then translated into often poetic Arabic. 'We try to put ourselves in the mind-set of someone receiving the message,' said Duncan MacInnes, the director of the Counterterrorism Communication Center, of which the bloggers are a part. 'Freedom for an Arab doesn't necessarily have the same meaning it has for an American. Honor does. So we might say terrorism is dishonorable, which resonates more.' (McFarquhar, 2007)

Another initiative from the same office is the Bloggers Roundtable, a series of conference calls where invited bloggers can speak with Pentagon officials about current issues. Sourcewatch cites a *Washington Post* article in which the director of new media operations at the US Office of the Assistant Secretary of Defense for Public Affairs, Roxie Merritt, explained that, 'while bloggers aren't being credentialed like media, the military is taking more time to communicate with bloggers to ensure that they post accurate information' (Sourcewatch, 2008, citing Schwab, 2007). In practice, according to an article in *Harper's Magazine*, the initiative is more about seeking 'to bypass the mainstream by working directly with a carefully culled list of military analysts, bloggers, and others who can be counted on to parrot the Bush Administration line on national security issues' (Silverstein, 2007).

At about the same time, other ways of intervening in the blogosphere were being talked about in military and political circles.

Wired magazine reports that in 2006 an academic at the Naval Postgraduate School proposed clandestinely recruiting bloggers: 'Hiring a block of bloggers to verbally attack a specific person or promote a specific message may be worth considering' (Denning, cited in Schachtman, 2008). Denning also suggested hacking into 'enemy blogs' and changing details so as to undermine their credibility or even to cause their authors to be regarded as traitors and 'taken down' by the enemy. It should be noted that a Special Operations Command spokesperson distanced the military from this 'academic exercise'. Yet Schulman (2006) provides evidence that the later abandoned Office of Strategic Influence (OSI) had been set up in 2001 with the aim of using the internet as part of US psychological operations in ways quite similar to those proposed by Denning. He cited a report by its director, Simon 'Pete' Worden, which proposed a range of propaganda tactics from the blatant – free music downloads or pornography to attract young Muslim men to websites carrying pro-US messages – to the more subtle:

> Discrediting extremist groups among foreign populations, Worden realized, would take 'respected authorities such as journalists, clerics and artists within that group to denounce' them. But 'simply paying them to do so is likely to boomerang,' he believed: 'Even if some can be so induced, the likely exposure of such tactics will do more to discredit our objectives than any gain achieved.' Therefore, 'a subtle mesh of inducements and disincentives must be developed. At the outset, we may offer free or increased access to the increasingly high technology means of communication ... to moderate voices.' (Ibid.: 42)

Schulman argues that, while the OSI was soon disbanded in 2002 under protest that its activities might include planting untrue stories in foreign media, it disappeared only in name – as indeed the then defense secretary, Donald Rumsfeld, stated publicly.

In the UK, there is less evidence of blogs being used as 'black propaganda' (a military term for information that appears to be from one source, but is actually from an opposing one).

However, the Ministry of Defence has closed down a number of blogs, proposing to offer in their place controlled spaces for soldiers to stay in contact with families and share their opinions. At the same time a ban on any communication by military personnel on 'issues arising from an individual's official business or experience' was issued. The ministry's director general of communications, Simon McDowell, told *The Guardian* that 'the MoD was experimenting with authorised blogs from Afghanistan . . . [and] was also seeking "legitimate outlets for people to express themselves"' (Gillan, 2007).

These initiatives come as no surprise. As new media emerge and evolve (Twitter is in the headlines at the time of writing), they are certain to attract the attention of those responsible for information management. The military's restrictions on letter-writing now extend to soldiers' blogs and e-mails. Each new effort to control what is said online, and by whom, is posited as a response to the use of the internet by radical groups intent on exploiting it for their purposes. For those concerned about the health of civil society, however, these and related initiatives are of pressing significance. Even in the most benign interpretation, they suggest that the most powerful countries in the world are actively extending the boundaries of public opinion management far beyond what would previously have been regarded as acceptable limits – or at least since the depths of the Cold War. Parallels with Orwellian surveillance overstate the case, but when there is 'strategic value' for officials to target individuals engaged in personal forms of communication such as blogs, the spaces available for independent thinking become steadily more constricted. The chilling effect becomes almost tangible, and self-censorship – as every journalist knows – is the most dangerous form of censorship of all.

This chapter has sought to show that the rise of micro-media produced by individuals situated outside of more traditional media contexts has been quickly followed by initiatives by media organizations – as well as by political and military interests – to reconcile them to their own agendas. In the process, the emergent ecology of digital war reporting has been shown to be evolving in complex ways, from the broadening of news organizations' resources to bear witness to atrocity to the collapsing, at times, of citizen media into state propaganda campaigns. Central to these struggles over representation has been the sudden proliferation of imagery, much of which is being produced through new forms and practices of photojournalism extended across the web. The next chapter, then, turns our attention to the digital image in wartime.

CHAPTER FIVE

Visual Truths: Images in Wartime

Introduction

Digital imagery of warfare is a routine, everyday feature of our news media. From a newspaper photograph's depiction of the tragedies of war in Iraq, to a news site's slideshow documenting the humanitarian crisis unfolding in Darfur, to a television newscast's video footage of the latest turn in the Israeli–Palestinian conflict, these images have a profound impact on our perceptions of the human condition. 'Being a spectator of calamities taking place in another country is a quintessential modern experience', maintained the late Susan Sontag (2003), 'the cumulative offering by more than a century and a half's worth of those professional, specialized tourists known as journalists.' This flow of pictures from distant places amounts to a torrent, featuring bloodshed at a seemingly ever-increasing rate. Sontag wrote:

> Parked in front of the little screens – television, computer, palmtop – we can surf to images and brief reports of disasters throughout the world. It seems as if there is a greater quantity of such news than before. This is probably an illusion. It's just that the spread of news is 'everywhere'. And some people's sufferings have a lot more intrinsic interest to an audience (given that suffering must be acknowledged as having an audience) than the suffering of others. (Ibid.: 16)

The response, she adds, varies from 'compassion, or indignation, or titillation, or approval, as each misery heaves into view' (ibid.).

For the photojournalist confronted with the challenge of bearing witness to conflict on our behalf, the effort to record human consequences is simultaneously one of interpretation, of assigning apposite meaning and relevance. The representation of violence, in other words, is partly constitutive of its reality, which makes this interpretive process acutely political. Important questions thus arise regarding 'our camera-mediated knowledge of war', to use Sontag's phrase, which will necessarily highlight the exercise of communicative power. 'Look, the photographs say, *this* is what it's like. This is what war *does*. And *that*, that is what it does, too', she observes. 'War tears, rends. War rips open, eviscerates. War scorches. War dismembers. War *ruins*' (Sontag, 2003: 7). Such imagery, it follows, invites a shared stance or point of view with the photographer, regardless of its implicit claim to be a 'record of the real', faithful to journalistic impartiality. The ways in which a photograph of an atrocity privileges a moment, effectively making 'real' events which 'we' might otherwise choose to ignore, is as much a question of framing (including but also, by definition, excluding) as it is of objectification. Such photographs 'give rise to opposing responses', Sontag points out. 'A call for peace. A cry for revenge. Or simply the bemused awareness, continually restocked by photographic information, that terrible things happen' (ibid.: 11–12). In each instance, photography makes possible the means to apprehend – at a distance – other people's pain, with all of the moral implications such a form of spectatorship engenders.

This chapter's discussion is informed by Sontag's perceptive engagement with the visual politics of suffering. In seeking to render problematic familiar assumptions about photojournalism in wartime, we shall examine the specific protocols of digital war photography in light of her critique. We begin in the next section by considering a controversial breach of journalistic ethics where the digital manipulation of news images is concerned, one which took place near Basra, Iraq, in March 2003, shortly after the US-led invasion was under way. A hastily made decision to 'tweak' an image, simply to improve its compositional balance, proved to have devastating consequences for the photojournalist in question (his career effectively destroyed) as his action ignited a debate that caught the attention of the world's press.

Digital dishonesty

Typically working under intense pressure, photojournalists in a war zone are recurrently forced to negotiate a range of formidable challenges. In the case of Brian Walski, a staff photographer (or 'shooter') for the *Los Angeles Times*, circumstances meant that he was in a state of near-exhaustion when on assignment in Basra, Iraq, in March 2003. In covering the movements of British troops, he came across a scene where a soldier was urging several Iraqi citizens to take cover from hostile gunfire, one of whom was holding a small child in his arms. Shooting digitally, Walski (2003) would later remember:

> Things are happening so fast. You have to watch out for yourself, and look what's going on to be able to compose pictures. I had ten frames of soldier totally cut off. At some point I must have zoomed out. When that guy came up with the baby, I shot off ten more frames. I had just one where you could see the soldier's face. The others he was turned away. (Walski, 2003)

At around 10pm that night, following what had become a fourteen-hour stint, he sat down with his laptop computer to review the day's work, deciding which photographs to relay back to the newsroom via the company's Newscom network. 'We were in Iraq at that point for six days', he recalled. 'We were sleeping in our car. . . . There was no safe haven of any kind where you could kind of relax and get a good night's sleep. It was constant tension.' This tension would later help to explain why Walski proceeded to make a decision that would bring his distinguished career to an abrupt end.

Sifting through the shots taken that day, Walski found himself 'playing around a little bit' in the effort to find a 'better image' in compositional terms. Since he had occasionally 'tweaked' photographs in the past ('taken out a phone pole') with image-editing software, it occurred to him that a merging of two of the shots would produce a more dramatic representation of events. In haste, he made a spur of the moment decision to 'improve' one image by digitally combining it with a second one – 'I put them together and thought, "Looks good," and that was it' – without pausing to think through the ramifications. In the composite version of the image, the British soldier appears to be cautioning the man holding the child, the imploring look of the Iraqi ostensibly giving expression to the tragic plight of innocent civilians caught up in the hostilities. Such a resonant photograph, not surprisingly, caught the attention of news editors, many of whom promptly cleared the space to run with it. The *LA Times* placed it on page 1, above the fold, while several other papers sharing syndication rights similarly gave it prominent play. Among the latter was the *Hartford Courant*, which positioned it across the width of the front page on 31 March 2003. The caption beneath it stated: 'A BRITISH SOLDIER from the Irish Guard orders fleeing Basra residents to get down near the Al Zubayr Bridge leading into the besieged city after their position came under fire from Iraqi forces holding the city Sunday.' A second line added: 'The civilians had gathered at the bridge, hoping to flee the city, when Iraqi paramilitaries opened fire on the British forces manning the bridge checkpoint', before directing the reader to the accompanying story on page A3. 'It was a great image', the *Courant*'s assistant managing editor for photography and graphics stated, 'and I missed the manipulation, and I feel bad for everyone involved' (cited in Irby, 2003).

It was another *Courant* employee, as it happened, who noticed that something seemed to be wrong with the photograph, namely the apparent duplication of figures in the background. Initial assumptions that there was some sort of technical glitch with the digital transmission via the satellite soon gave way to the painful realization that this was a deliberate attempt to deceive (a 600 per cent magnification in Photoshop helped to reveal the evidence). Walski, still in southern Iraq, was contacted by telephone and asked for an explanation. Evidently he did not hesitate to admit what he had done, and offered to resign. Managers at the *LA Times*, while sympathetic to his personal predicament, moved decisively to fire him for what they considered to be a serious breach of trust with the paper's readers. An 'Editor's note', placed within a box in the bottom right-hand corner of the front page, was published in the next edition. It stated:

> On Monday, March 31, the Los Angeles Times published a front-page photograph that had been altered in violation of Times policy.
>
> The primary subject of the photo was a British soldier directing Iraqi civilians to take cover from Iraqi fire on the outskirts of Basra. After publication, it was noticed that several civilians in the background appear twice. The photographer, Brian Walski, reached by telephone in southern Iraq, acknowledged that he had used his computer to combine elements of two photographs, taken moments apart, in order to improve the composition.
>
> Times policy forbids altering the content of news photographs. Because of the violation, Walski, a Times photographer since 1998, has been dismissed from the staff. The altered photo, along with the two photos that were used to produce it, is published today on A6. (*Los Angeles Times*, 2 April 2003)[*]

A policy forbidding the alteration of news photographs was also in place at the *Courant*, where staff members were reportedly crestfallen to learn that it had been violated. 'This is a huge embarrassment to the industry', one of its staff photographers stated at the time. 'This sort of thing damages the credibility of all of us', he added. 'Once you've lost your trust, you might as well be selling aluminum siding' (cited in M. McCarthy, 2003).

Reactions to this 'digital deception' – as it was described in some accounts – received attention in press reports around the globe, and sparked considerable debate within the blogosphere. Further insight into the situation was provided by one of Walski's former colleagues at the *LA Times*, photographer Don Bartletti, who had seen him shortly after the shots were taken. 'He is my friend and I respect the heroic images that he made and the tremendous effort that he has contributed', he told Poynter Online from Kuwait City. 'When I saw him, I really did not recognize him. He was sunburned, had not eaten in days, nor slept in 36

---

[*]   (The two original images and the composite version can be found online, including at junipermedia.net/nucleus/index.php?itemid=32).

hours, his clothes were filthy, his beard – all over the place. And he smelled like a goat' (cited in Irby, 2003). Other photojournalists weighed in to describe the extent to which the stress of working in a war zone, coupled with sleep deprivation, can lead to a state of mental exhaustion whereby lapses in professionalism become more likely (Walski, in an apology e-mailed to the entire photography staff at the *LA Times*, readily acknowledged his 'complete breakdown in judgment'). Intense competition among photojournalists, fuelled by adrenaline and a keen sense of rivalry, was cited as a further contributory factor. 'It's about beating the other guy', stated photo editor Jim Mahoney of the *Boston Herald*. 'But sometimes in an effort to make that moment, you can lose sight of the picture . . . the big picture, as well as the one in front of you' (cited in Gelzinis, 2003). Still others pointed to the type of temptation engendered by digital technology itself – that is, the ease with which photojournalists in the field can perform 'touch ups' on images to 'clean' away 'noise' or to achieve better 'balance'. Walski's transgression, some suggested, was that he took aesthetic matters too far. His desire to compose an image that was pleasing to the eye meant that he overstepped a boundary, thereby calling into question the integrity of the image itself as an accurate reflection of reality. 'Any time you make up anything at all, you shouldn't be working at a newspaper', *LA Times* managing editor Dean Baquet told the *Washington Post*. 'He made this picture something we're not even sure occurred. He heightened the drama of the picture. It's like changing a quote to make it more dramatic' (cited in Kurtz, 2003).

The actual extent to which any digital image can reflect reality was called into question by other commentators, however. Accusations of 'electronic doctoring' risk concealing the fact that the use of software to convert shots is unavoidable, given the basic steps followed by photographers in processing a digital image – often shot in a fine JPEG and RAW file (sometimes called a 'digital negative') simultaneously – into a format that can be viewed back in the newsroom. Data within the RAW version is processed to a minimal degree by the camera's image sensor so as to ensure that as much information is retained as possible for purposes of manipulation – pixels being adjusted for contrast, sharpening, white balancing, colour grading or saturation, and so forth – prior to the image being converted into TIFF or JPEG formats for e-mailing or printing. In this context, an analogy is sometimes drawn with respect to the processing of film in the darkroom – a RAW file being, in effect, the digital equivalent of the exposed film negative awaiting processing. Disputes over what is permissible by way of alteration thus revolve, to some extent, over standards set down in relation to a pre-digital medium. That is to say, a language of film permeates normative descriptions of what sort of practical adjustments can be safely regarded as reasonable and appropriate. Techniques such as cropping, tinting, dodging or burning, once painstakingly applied through an elaborate set of procedures in a news organization's darkroom in order to accentuate the news photograph's intended significance (if not 'editorial message'), can now be realized in a matter of minutes through a series of keystrokes and/or clicks of a mouse on a laptop computer in the field. Seemingly straightforward policy statements forbidding 'altering the content of news photographs' thus tend to gloss over the subtle ways in which images are routinely crafted in order to enhance their quality for better reproduction, thereby appearing to make what is really a question of emphasis into a stark either/or proposition.

These issues suggested an alternative understanding of the Walski controversy in the eyes of some critics. Given these technical constraints, they insisted, it is necessary to dispel once and for all the illusion that the news photograph can be objective (the promise of the digital image to be more 'truthful' in its representation than its film predecessor being untenable, in their view). Photographer Pedro Meyer, for example, maintained that the *LA Times* lacked a valid reason for dismissing Walski. The content of the composite image, he believed, had not been altered in its essence. In his words:

> they have fired someone for doing a professional job in trying to come up with a better picture, the same way that any of their

journalists polish a text so that it reads better and is succinct. (Why should a photographer be deprived of doing exactly the same that other professionals are doing on a daily basis as long as the information is not distorted?) The only explanation I can find, is that by accusing the photographer and attempting to portray themselves as publishing 'unmanipulated' news, they are seeking to conceal the factual reality of their biased and one-sided presentation of the overall news. That seems to be the more important issue at hand. (Meyer, 2003)

For Meyer, the more significant concern was the attempt made by the *LA Times* to use this issue as a smokescreen of sorts, one intended to cover up 'the wholesale abdication of their responsibility in bringing to the public any news other than what the Pentagon or the White House wishes them to publish'. This line of defence was quickly challenged by other critics, however, such as Frank Van Riper (2003), writing on the *Washington Post*'s Camera Works site. In his opinion, Meyer was simply wrong to suggest that a professional journalist would 'polish' a direct quote from a source. 'Remember', he admonished Meyer, '*news photographs are the equivalent of direct quotations* and therefore are sacrosanct – the situational ethics of Walski's apologists notwithstanding.' A reputable photojournalist will make various technical adjustments to a digital image, but would never alter its 'key elements'. These elements, in his view, 'like the key words in a direct quote, simply are off limits to manipulation'.

Transgressing boundaries

The limits of manipulation, as the above example so effectively illustrates, tend to be easier to discern when they are transgressed than would be the case under ordinary circumstances. Differing views about whether Walski was guilty of changing the essential meaning of the image continued to simmer for some time afterwards, but the overwhelming consensus among newspaper commentators held that his actions were to be condemned. Even where it was acknowledged that there was no such thing as an undoctored, unmanipulated digital image, the perceived tenets of professionalism dictated that certain (largely tacit) rules be respected regarding what qualifies as acceptable conduct (as Van Riper (2003) recalled one newspaper's admonition to its digital photographers: 'If you can't do it in the darkroom, don't do it here').

To the extent that this distinction amounts to a moral code, its invocation is intended to police a boundary between practical adaptation and deliberate fabrication. No concession is made for extenuating circumstances, even in wartime. '[It] is precisely because so much of the most important journalism is done under such intense pressure that absolute standards are required', stated Tim Rutten (2003), media critic at the *LA Times*. 'You don't want reporters with bullets flying over their heads or minutes to their deadlines parsing the moral ambiguities of their craft.' That said, however, principled values will be certain to prove contingent upon the ad hoc negotiation of conflicting pressures. Digital photojournalism, by its very nature, decisively recasts familiar film-based criteria, not least by making possible a near-instantaneous – from the battlefield to the picture desk – turnaround time. Mark Edward Harris recalls a telling example from the Second World War by way of contrast:

> In 1944, Robert Capa went ashore with the first wave at Omaha Beach. He relayed film back to one of the ships offshore and it was rushed to New York for special processing. Several hours later, a group of editors at *Life* Magazine gathered around a table as a lab tech hurriedly dried the negatives that showed the very first images of the Allied invasion at Normandy. The viewers, including the lab tech, were so transfixed by what they saw that they froze, and in so doing, the heat gun that was drying the negatives got too close and the emulsion melted, leaving only a handful of photographs intact. (When *Life* published the surviving photographs, it claimed the blurry look was because Capa's hands were shaking.) (Harris, 2003)

A photojournalist in Afghanistan or Iraq today, equipped with a laptop computer and a satellite telephone, can transmit an image minutes after it has been shot. Patrick Whalen, assignment editor at Getty Images, underscores the demands of time pressure when describing the 'live wire feed' from the war zone. Once the images arrive, he explained, any 'minor adjustments' are made in Photoshop as quickly as possible so as to avoid a delay in distribution. 'Our turnaround time to get the images out to our subscription clients, which are mostly newspapers and magazines, is around 15 minutes', he stated. 'That's compared to taking several hours just a couple of years ago' (cited ibid.).

The perceived benefits of the heightened speed and immediacy rendered achievable by digital photojournalism – crucial when the competition for media space is so fierce – may nonetheless raise concerns about accountability when editorial processes are being effectively streamlined. This may take the explicit form discussed above with regard to the Walski case (inviting speculation about the number of altered images that have escaped detection thus far), but arguably even more insidious are the subtle ways in which such imagery encourages a particular stance or point of view. Photojournalists 'embedded' with US or British troops in Afghanistan and Iraq have evidently welcomed the mobility afforded by portable digital technologies (the capacity to relay images while travelling, for example, being a critical consideration when personal safety is threatened), yet recognize that the sheer range and volume of such images risks denying them sufficient explanatory context. Moreover, what the 'embed' gains by way of access to the war zone is countered, in turn, by a corresponding loss of journalistic independence (in contrast to the relative freedoms enjoyed by the 'unilaterals'). The photographs taken almost always reflect the unit's perspective – hardly surprising when survival depended on maintaining a positive relationship with its members. Thorne Anderson, speaking of his time as an embedded photojournalist in Iraq, states:

> Some journalists have done great work while embedded, but the perspective of embedded journalists is very limited. They only see what the troops see, and they only get to meet ordinary Iraqis on rare occasions and always surrounded by soldiers,

guns, and heavy armor. It's impossible to see Iraq from a more local perspective under those circumstances. Embedding with the military is a great way to do a story about the soldiers and the effect the war has on them, but it's not the best way to report on what this war has done to Iraq. . . . I felt like I was trapped in a heavily armored plastic bubble. I could see Iraq from the back seat of those humvees, but I couldn't touch it or feel it or interact with it. And it was impossible to have any kind of meaningful contact with Iraqi people while wearing body armor and surrounded by American soldiers. (Cited in Komp, 2006)

Fellow photojournalist Rita Leistner concurs. Working as an embedded photojournalist in Iraq for four months in 2003, she was routinely frustrated in her attempts to record the terrible effects of the war on ordinary Iraqi citizens. The situation became even worse in the succeeding years, in her view. 'Today in Iraq', she states, 'it is impossible to work as an unembedded journalist without it being a near suicidal act' (cited ibid.).

Under these circumstances, it is understandable why some of the most memorable – even iconic – photographs of the Iraq War have been taken by amateurs. 'With the technology now, the amateur photographer is as capable as a professional journalist and is operating with the same tools: digital camera, laptop and an Internet connection', observed Keith W. Jenkins, photo editor of the *Washington Post Magazine*. 'The embedded process was supposed to give government a better handle on what journalists were doing, but now you have this whole rogue operation of civilians with digital cameras who have access to things the media don't' (cited in Simon, 2004). The poignant rawness of many 'amateur' images throws into sharp relief the ways in which 'professionalism' has been recurrently aligned with the type of sanitized imagery preferred by military minders. In addition to becoming 'beholden to the military for access and safety', Fred Ritchin (2004) maintains, the professional photographer has been forced to be 'responsive to back-home publications that wanted to tell the war in a "patriotic" way' – the result being that 'some critical judgment seems to have been ceded'.

An image the US government did not want its citizens to see, taken by Tami Silicio, an employee of a freight company in Kuwait and e-mailed to the *Seattle Times* (April 2004). © T. Silico. Used with permission

The vital contribution amateur photographers are making to the visual mediation of the war is being increasingly recognized. One especially noteworthy instance, which helped to crystallize both public and journalistic concerns about the imagery of the Iraq War, occurred in April 2004. The *Seattle Times* was able to print a photograph of military coffins being transported back from Iraq – the type of image the Pentagon had banned from media publication, ostensibly out of respect for the privacy of dead soldiers' families – because a civilian working in Kuwait International Airport, Tami Silicio, had e-mailed a shot taken on her digital Nikon Coolpix (3.2 megapixel) camera to a friend back in the US. The shot in question showed rows of flag-draped coffins being secured into place on an air force cargo plane. Her friend, Amy Katz, forwarded it to Barry Fitzsimmons, photo editor at the *Seattle Times* (Silicio's hometown newspaper). When the photograph arrived, 'I just said wow', Fitzsimmons recalled.

'The picture was something we don't have access to as the media' (cited in Fancher, 2004a). In recognizing its extraordinary news value, he also knew that it was 'too powerful an image just to drop into the newspaper' without first establishing the story behind it. Following several e-mails and telephone calls between Silicio and Fitzsimmons (and later staff reporter Hal Bernton), the decision was taken to publish one of the images on the front page of the Sunday edition under the headline: 'The somber task of honoring the fallen'. The opening paragraph of Bernton's account reads:

> The aluminum boxes, in ordered rows, are bound by clean white straps on freshly scrubbed pallets. American flags are draped evenly over the boxes. Uniformed honor guards form on either side of the pallets as they move from the tarmac to the entryways of the cargo planes. There are prayers, salutes and hands on hearts. Then the caskets are carefully placed in cargo holds for a flight to Germany. (Bernton, 2004)

The account proceeds to point out that the loading of caskets has become a ritual performed over and over again in recent weeks, before quoting Silicio herself commenting on how everyone involved salutes the fallen service members with 'such emotion and intensity and respect'. It was a ritual, she believed, the families would be proud to see.

In electing to run the photograph, news editors at the *Seattle Times* were aware that they would be contravening a policy adopted by the Pentagon in 1991, during the first Gulf War, to prohibit news organizations from photographing coffins at military bases. They similarly knew that the photograph was likely to spark strong reactions from readers, not all of whom would agree with the newspaper's position. 'We're not making a statement about the course of the war', Fitzsimmons stated at the time. 'Readers will make their own sense of the picture, their own judgment' (cited in Fancher, 2004b).

The magnitude of the ensuing controversy caught everyone by surprise, it seemed, with the image promptly reproduced across the mediascape – including on the front pages of several other newspapers around the country. Matters intensified even further when Silicio was abruptly fired from her job in the cargo terminal two days later. Press accounts pointed to 'avalanching public opinion' when describing the 'onslaught of media requests for the photo' and the 'blizzard of media inquiries' into what had happened (*Seattle Times* editors found themselves being interviewed extensively, on programmes such as 'Good Morning America' and 'NBC Nightly News', over several days). Maytag Aircraft Corporation, the employer of Silicio and her husband, claimed that her action was in breach of both company and base disclosure rules (its president was widely quoted as stating that the military had identified 'very specific concerns'). The *Seattle Times* expressed its regret about her dismissal. 'I'm happy the picture is out', Fitzsimmons stated, 'but it broke my heart when I found out she lost her job' (cited in Geraci, 2004a). The paper had alerted Silicio about possible risks when obtaining her permission to use the image, having rightly anticipated that there might be repercussions, but remained steadfast in the face of criticism. Managing editor David Boardman insisted that his paper's motives – like those of Silicio herself – were honourable, and there was no anti-war agenda at work. '[We] weren't attempting to convey any sort of political message', he explained, before expressing his disagreement with the military ban. 'The Administration cannot tell us what we can and cannot publish' (cited in Overington, 2004). Jim Vesely, the paper's editorial page director, described how 'dumbfounded' staffers were by the public response from around the world – 'at one point the e-mails were coming at one per second' – and how much they appreciated what were 'overwhelmingly positive' reactions on the whole (cited in Fancher, 2004b).

The uproar continued to escalate as a diverse array of voices weighed into the controversy. Interpretations of the photograph's significance varied dramatically, often passionately so. Appeals to freedom of expression clashed with protests that the photo was undermining the war effort. Newspaper headlines highlighted key themes, such as the photograph's emotional power ('The photo that stirred a nation', *Seattle Times*), its legality ('Pentagon ban on pictures of dead troops is broken', *New York Times*) and its subversive quality ('Sacked for photo Americans weren't meant to see', *Sydney Morning Herald*), among other aspects. Democratic Party presidential candidate John Kerry praised Silicio's action, maintaining that the public had the right to see such images, while President Bush reaffirmed his belief in the rightness of the military ban. Disputes over whether the ban constituted censorship figured prominently, with many critics outraged by what they considered to be yet another instance of the determination of the Pentagon and Bush administration to control public perceptions of the conflict. 'This was an effort by the Pentagon to do what they have so often done, which was try to control the media', Tom Jarriel, former correspondent for ABC News, argued. 'They try to prevent Americans from seeing the toll that the war is taking in terms of graphic pictures, so that they don't lose public support for the war' (Deborah Norville Tonight, 2004). The presumed capacity of Silicio's photograph to set alight public opinion was shared by both pro- and anti-war voices, despite their inability to agree on much else. 'The image of dead Americans, especially the dead American soldier, is probably the most powerful image of war for Americans', stated critic David Perlmutter. 'It's the one that immediately strikes us in the gut, because we hate to see it but we recognize we may need to see it' (cited in Rivera, 2004). Meanwhile, upon her return from Kuwait, Silicio expressed her own growing scepticism about the case for war. 'The newspapers have opened my eyes to what that picture meant for everyone in the nation', she told *Editor & Publisher* magazine. 'I didn't realize how censored the United States has been on what's going on in Iraq' (cited in Geraci, 2004b).

Although photographs of war and its aftermath have been taken by amateurs since the earliest days of the medium, suddenly it seemed that digitally generated imagery was being heralded – or, more typically, criticized – for its transformative potential. 'In an era when pictures and video can be captured and distributed across the world with a few clicks', Amy Harmon (2004) observed in the *New York Times*, 'the traditional establishment – the military, the government, the mainstream media – appears to be losing control of the images of war.' Digital technology, she proceeds to point out, 'is forcing a major shift in the expectation of what can be kept private, and it may ultimately hold everyone more accountable for their actions.' In addition to the Silicio case, the examples she cites include a website (TheMemoryHole.org) which posted further images of military coffins being shipped from Iraq (obtained via a Freedom of Information request), the grisly video of Nicholas Berg being decapitated by extremists, and various social networking sites where war images circulate. Most important in this regard, however, were the photographs of Iraqi prisoners being abused by their American captors in the notorious Abu Ghraib prison 20 miles outside Baghdad. Despite the concerted efforts of human rights groups to draw news media attention to the disturbing allegations being made regarding the US military's mistreatment of Iraqi prisoners, their information was all but ignored by journalists for several months. Everything would change when digital images casually snapped by soldiers inside Abu Ghraib, effectively documenting the maltreatment on an unimagined scale, found their way into the hands of the mainstream media.

Visual truth-telling

Since the early 2000s, digital cameras, camcorders and camera phones have become part of the everyday culture of US and other Western militaries (Simon, 2004), near ubiquitous in ordinary soldiers' kit bags. The vast majority of the images recorded by these military personnel appear to be innocuous snaps or amateur videos, e-mailed home or posted on websites to connect with families and friends, or shared within barracks or on military websites. A glance at a site such as Militaryphotos.net shows many thousands of shots of soldiers posing alongside their equipment or in their living quarters. A few, however, display aspects of military life that contrast starkly with the official image of the occupying forces. In particular, 'trophy images' – images of dead or injured enemy, sometimes involving posing with the body, even in rare cases cutting off the head or limbs or otherwise abusing the body, that in past wars would seldom have been viewed by more than a handful of people – can be found among the snapshots, celebrating not just victory but the total power of the victor.

During the US-led wars in Iraq and Afghanistan, such 'kill-zone' imagery has found a wider, though still limited, audience on specialist interest websites, among them 'amateur porn' services that allow soldiers to exchange graphic images for access to pornography (one of the most notorious 'bodies-for-porn' sites, NTFU, operated for over two years before it was closed for violating Florida felony obscenity laws). To some, the interrelated worlds of violence and pornography revealed in this circulation of digital images exposed basic truths about war. One critic, writing on the communal blog Metafilter about the porn for trophy-image exchange, stated:

> [T]his is the perfect collection of anti-war photos. War is incredibly ugly, and the current administration has done (for their party) a superb job of sanitzing [*sic*] anything the least bit objectionable or graphic. This solves that. The human costs of war must be told, and the American public being the thick-headed fools that most of them are, told in the most graphic, bread-and-circuses form. (NucleophilicAttack, 2005)

The image of war is suddenly out of the hands of the political marketer or the cautious editor and in the hands of others – among them soldiers, citizens, activists. The circulation of images taken by such people happens in a way that appears at times to cut across a view of war as tidy or morally comfortable (thereby undermining efforts to construct the 'virtuous war' (Der Derian, 2001) discussed in chapter 1).

In one sense, it should be noted, there is nothing new about such imagery. The Spanish–American war of 1898, Susan Moeller points out, 'had three or four soldiers who brought their brand-new Kodaks to the front' (Moeller, 1989: xiii). Professional photographers, since the earliest days of the technology, have also recorded images which have fuelled accusations of atrocity in war. What distinguishes war imagery in a digital culture, as the Silicio photograph reveals, is the speed with which such images are transmitted. As a result, they become very quickly inserted into different contexts, including into wider public debate about the conflict from which they arise. Soldiers' private snaps may become public documents at any moment; practices usually tightly constrained by military regulation and segregation are exhibited for reinterpretation by others, such as the Metafilter blogger above. In a process which appears anarchic to politicians and journalists alike, these pictures are trophies of war one moment, entertainment the next, then pornography and finally evidence of the 'truth' of war, among other possibilities. Moreover, digital snaps from the war zone appear sometimes to be viewed and interpreted in ways distinct from images that have been purposely taken for public consumption. On a number of occasions during the conflicts in Afghanistan and Iraq, soldiers' images not intended as public documents were treated as more authentic, more credible and ultimately better records of what was 'really happening' than the accounts of military or political figures – or, for that matter, the images of professional photojournalists. They have become, one journalist wrote, 'the unofficial "true" record of the war' (Friedman, 2006). As with much citizen journalism, the lure of the soldier's digital image is that it differs in some essential way from professional journalism or other 'official' genres.

The photoblog of Sean Dustman, a medical corpsman in the US Navy serving in Iraq and a self-confessed 'shutterbug', illustrates the phenomenon. Dustman started a photoblog six months before he was sent to Iraq in early 2004. Once there, his site became, he said later, something of an unofficial record of his unit after he received repeated requests from his fellow Marines for copies of his photographs. Soon the pages at dustmans.photoblog.com – containing nearly 4,000 images in the first year alone – were attracting soldiers' relatives seeking both evidence that their loved ones were safe and some vicarious contact with them (Hebert, 2004). Of particular interest is that Dustman's photoblog – along with the text blog he also kept – seems to have taken on a number of roles at once. It was the place to put the results of his photography; it was a record for his troop of Marines; it was a form of interpersonal communication; and it was also read by some as a form of journalism – particularly after television interviews, blogger awards and the republication of some of his entries in a book of military bloggers gave him a high public profile. The way Dustman's blog flitted in and out of the public eye, which was far from unique, brought the personal dimension of those recording their participation in conflict to the forefront of public awareness.

The repercussions of this movement between front and back spaces very soon became apparent in Iraq, in a quite spectacular way. 'Images define wars', as Jerry Lanson (2003) points out. 'So if war looks like a Fourth of July fireworks display over Baghdad', he writes, members of the public 'are a lot more likely to feel an energizing, if uneasy, excitement at the "shock and awe" of US military might than if war looks, for example, like a frightened American captive.' Lanson's observation, made in March 2003 when the Al Jazeera network provoked outrage in the West with its decision to broadcast footage of captured American soldiers, proved equally telling a year later when the captives concerned were Iraqi. Digital photographs of terrified Iraqi prisoners being tortured by US soldiers in the notorious Abu Ghraib prison shattered the norms of Pentagon-sanctioned imagery at a stroke.

'These unbelievable photographs'

To date, no so-called amateur imagery has engendered a greater impact on public perceptions of war than the shots of US soldiers abusing their prisoners. Secretary of State Donald Rumsfeld expressed his exasperation when called to account for their actions before Congress:

Private First Class Lynndie England poses with a naked prisoner in one of the digital photographs of torture at Abu Ghraib prison, near Baghdad (early 2004). © Rex Features.

> We're functioning with peacetime constraints, with legal requirements, in a wartime situation, in the Information Age, where people are running around with digital cameras and taking these unbelievable photographs and then passing them off, against the law, to the media, to our surprise, when they had not even arrived in the Pentagon. (Cited in PBS, 2004)

The story of the Abu Ghraib images is one of a powerful form of representation outside of the knowledge and therefore control of those in authority. Yet it is also a story of the fragility of that representation in the face of established practices of representing war. Briefly, news about what was happening inside the prison broke when the CBS News programme *60 Minutes II* went on air on 28 April 2004 with several of the horrific images in its possession. In the course of the ensuing furore, CBS was widely heralded for its shocking exclusive. Closer scrutiny of its handling of the story, though, revealed that the programme's producers had provided

Pentagon officials with ample opportunity to prepare a 'media response' (some eleven pages in length) before the images were broadcast. Specifically, details emerged that, eight days before the report was to air, CBS anchor Dan Rather had been contacted by General Richard B. Myers, chair of the Joint Chiefs of Staff, requesting that the broadcast be delayed, if not suspended altogether. Myers reportedly expressed his concerns about the potential repercussions for US forces in Iraq, fearing that the release of the images might result in further deaths of soldiers.

Few would dispute that it was understandable for Pentagon officials to be making such a request of CBS News, given their interest in 'managing' the crisis. Far less comprehensible, in the opinion of critics, was CBS's decision to grant it. Evidently, when *60 Minutes II* finally went to air, their primary motivation was to pre-empt Seymour Hersh's (2004) report on the prisoner abuse – complete with photographs – which they had heard was about to be published by the *New Yorker* magazine. Many of those who had been dismayed by CBS's apparent willingness to bow to Pentagon pressure were quick to speculate about what might have happened otherwise. Had CBS not feared being scooped by Hersh, would it have broadcast a less substantive treatment of events, or even elected to hold the story back altogether? Rather himself had explained to viewers why the request was granted in a 'postscript' to the story:

> A postscript. Two weeks ago, we received an appeal from the Defense Department, and eventually from the chairman of the military Joint Chiefs of Staff, General Richard Myers, to delay this broadcast given the danger and tension on the ground in Iraq. We decided to honor that request while pressing for the Defense Department to add its perspective to the incidents at Abu Ghraib Prison. This week, with the photos beginning to circulate elsewhere and with other journalists about to publish their versions of the story, the Defense Department agreed to cooperate in our report. (*60 Minutes II*, CBS TV, 28 April 2004)

Jeff Fager, executive producer of *60 Minutes II*, later insisted that he felt 'terrible' about the delay. 'News is a delicate thing', he stated. 'It's hard to just make those kinds of decisions. It's not natural for us; the natural thing is to put it on the air. But the circumstances were quite unusual, and I think you have to consider that' (cited in *Washington Post*, 4 May 2004). Many critics were less than convinced, to put it mildly, arguing that there was no justification for suppressing the story. Some believed that defence officials' agreement to 'co-operate' signalled little more than a desire to 'spin' the story in a manner that would help contain adverse publicity.

The scandal, according to the official line, revolved around the actions of some 'bad apples', and was not indicative of systemic policies and procedures. Evidence to the contrary was readily available elsewhere, of course, not least with respect to the abuses committed in Afghanistan and Guantánamo Bay. Meanwhile there could be no denying the sad reality that two weeks of CBS self-censorship must have had painful consequences for the Iraqi prisoners in question. These snapshots from digital cameras, saved onto CDs and passed around prison staff, showed the physical and sexual abuse of Iraqi prisoners in shocking detail. In one, a guard used an Alsatian dog to menace a cowering, naked man. In another, naked men were piled on top of each other to simulate group sex while a guard took a photo. In another, a bruised corpse lay wrapped in cellophane, with a smiling guard posing beside it, giving the thumbs up. In perhaps the most infamous of them, a thin, hooded figure stood atop a box, arms out-stretched, with electrodes dangling from his fingers. In the *New Yorker*, investigative journalist Seymour Hersh claimed that some of the prisoners in the images were raped and at least one was tortured until he died. Soon, he and journalists at other publications were able to gather textual evidence showing that the incidents were not exceptional, but examples of routine violent and degrading treatment of prisoners in the prison and elsewhere.

It is hard to overstate the importance of these images, not just because of their longer term symbolic impact on public perceptions (and later memory) of the occupation of Iraq, but also because they underlined the enormous power of private digital images in certain cases, here allowing a hitherto suppressed and denied story of systemic abuse to emerge. Human rights organizations had reported severe human rights abuses in prisons in Iraq a year earlier, and in Afghanistan and Guantánamo Bay before that, but few Western news outlets, and almost none in the US, had picked up on their concerns. The whistleblower who was CBS's initial source for its Abu Ghraib story later said he had been rebuffed by many politicians and journalists before *60 Minutes II* took up the story (Dao and Lichtblau, 2004). A number of correspondents in Baghdad admitted later that they had been approached by Iraqis with stories and evidence of torture at the hands of US soldiers, but had done little further research on the claims and rarely published them. Anthony Shadid, Islamic affairs correspondent for the *Washington Post*, remembered:

> People would show us the scars of handcuffs on their hands, whatever, the bruised backs, and I don't think we pursued them nearly as rigorously as we should have. I think it's very difficult to prove who's beaten somebody. (Cited in CJR, 2006: 38)

Stories of other abuses, including strong evidence that US troops stood by as Afghan forces executed up to 3,000 Taliban prisoners, individual deaths of prisoners at US military prisons, and the 'extraordinary rendition' by the US of prisoners to third countries where torture was used, had been similarly 'buried, played down or ignored' by editors and reporters in the US. These accounts were typically deemed implausible, and most certainly unpalatable, in a country where mainstream journalism had become narrowly patriotic in the aftermath of the September 11 attacks (Umansky, 2006; Zelizer and Allan, 2002).

One of the conditions enabling journalists finally to report the story was that an official paper trail substantiated them. The Pentagon had known of the images from the Baghdad prison since at least January 2004, three months before the *60 Minutes II* and *New Yorker* stories. Leaked copies of its reports into the abuse added to the impact of both stories, allowing reporters to confirm both the abuse and its systemic nature. Umansky (2006: 21) quotes an Associated Press correspondent, Charles Hanley, whose stories six months earlier of similar military abuse of Iraqis had languished because they lacked such official confirmation; they remained simply accusations by individual Iraqis, who were regarded by many editors as untrustworthy enemy combatants. By April 2004, reporters could underpin their evidence with the military's own reports. But it was clearly the shocking visual evidence of torture – the pictures themselves – that made the story compelling. O'Neill notes that CNN admitted dropping another story on prisoner abuse because, 'without having the actual photos to hand, "this was not such a big story"' (O'Neill, 2004). The Abu Ghraib images allowed these allegations to become facts for Western journalists.

The pictures' status as a particular kind of fact, then, lies at the heart of how this story – when so many others were abandoned or neglected – became powerful. Zelizer's (2005) description of the news image's twin status within journalism's understanding of itself is a useful starting point in exploring this power. She notes that photographs appear to stand not only as a particularly powerful form of evidence for journalists but also as pegs on which larger, more abstract meanings are hung. Thus they are better able than words to act as eyewitness testimony connecting the viewer with the event and compelling public attention. The Abu Ghraib images indeed stood as incontrovertible evidence, able to refute claims by the US military that its employees did not use torture. One commentator argued after the scandal broke that, 'in an era when there is less trust of the media than there has been in the past, where print and audio can leave people unmoved, a photo has tremendous impact, because it's evidence' (Jurkowitz, 2004). On the other hand, Zelizer (2005) argues that images are more often used by news organizations to support and illustrate written text. Photographs tend to have the status of the typical or the conventional, and so become a 'tool for interpreting events in ways consonant with long-standing understandings about the world' (Zelizer, 2005: 28; see also Zelizer, 2002). A number of commentators argue that the Abu Ghraib images made sense in such ideological terms. They recalled for some the atrocity image genre dating back to the Belgian Congo or Nazi death camps (Sliwinski, 2006), thereby placing the US-led invasion intertextually in quite different ways to official imagery (and to claims that the Bush administration and its allies were bringing freedom and civilization to Iraq). 'It is difficult to imagine a worse propaganda defeat', stated one editorial writer (Kelly, 2004; see also Ahluwalia, 2006).

However, as important as the ability of these photographs to convey a particular truth about the US invasion of Iraq was their origin as digital snapshots sent by guards to their friends and colleagues. This gave them a twofold power. Firstly, as Sontag (2004) has argued, these were messages as much as objects. The acts of photographing and then sending images to other soldiers by e-mail or on CDs were acts of participation in a shared world. To outsiders, the meanings they trailed as they moved from that private world to the public space of the news page signalled a military culture in which fear, hatred, violence and comradeship were mixed and whose pleasures reflected that mixture. For it was the attitudes that lay behind the acts of taking these photographs, the deliberate posing of victims in order to abuse them further by recording their humiliation, that horrified many commentators. Viewing these images was thus to come much closer to the torture than viewing photographs taken, for example, by a third party such as a human rights worker or journalist. It was to hear at first hand a message of sadism and dehumanization – indeed, Malik (2006) argues that an element of excitement is mixed in with viewing such illicit images. As large numbers of other pictures and abuse stories were made public in the following year, a military subculture became apparent in which soldiers traded in images of violence against Iraqis, the Taliban and others. As home-made DVDs such as 'Ramadi Madness', a compilation of trophy images shot by reservists after a tour in the dangerous city of Ramadi, and image-sharing websites such as NTFU.com, LiveLeak and Under Mars came to public knowledge, a picture of a systemic disrespect for others' lives or cultures among some in the US military and its allies became clear.

Secondly, and related to the first point, the images were private. Because they were not intended for public consumption, they appeared separate from the efforts of those seeking to direct public debate and were therefore more 'authentic' voices from the war zone. Thus we must be cautious in assessing claims that the Abu Ghraib images are evidence of a 'digital democratization', in which new technologies are 'letting little people make big waves. During World War II, US prison guards didn't have the power to flood their government with bad publicity. And in Saddam Hussein's Iraq, abused prisoners had no chance of seeing their plight vividly brought to the world's attention' (Wright, 2004). For the images were taken, later reports suggested, for multiple reasons: as personal records of the guards' work, to humiliate the prisoners so as to weaken their resolve to resist interrogation – read torture – efforts, and to entertain the guards. It was precisely the fact, then, that they were not motivated by an intention to 'make waves' in public that gave the images their power. Accompanying knowledge about the secret and sadistic world of which they were part, and the fact that they had come to public light against their authors' wishes, provided a good deal of their meaning.

Werbach, pointing to the rapidity with which the images circulated among US bloggers, contends that the Abu Ghraib scandal signalled the growing power of this media form. These images, he writes, 'weren't first leaked or published by blogs but the fact that blogs got wind of them and pointed to them made the news spread like wildfire'. As a result, he adds, '[a]nybody, including the White House and the executive suite, who feels it's important to limit the flow of information is going to have to deal with how blogs are now making that harder' (cited in Hunter and Werbach, 2005: 18). However, others maintain that the Abu Ghraib images did not have an immediate political impact in the US. It was in their wider circulation, through Arab news channels, blogs and propagandist collections of horror images on CDs, that they grew into a major challenge to the legitimacy of the US occupation. Umansky (2006: 22) notes that an initial lack of interest in concerns about torture from the Republican-dominated Congress and a subdued news media led to 'scattered sprinkles' of coverage there. Images which conflicted so utterly with the official scripts which until then had dominated news coverage were perhaps difficult to report on, allowing the Bush administration's framing of the story as one of 'a few bad apples', rather than as a widespread policy of abuse, to prevail (Andén-Papadopoulos, 2008; Danner, 2004). In Europe, coverage was more extensive, but it was in Arab media that the images received heaviest coverage. There the photographs and accompanying news articles reinforced already widespread stories of abuse, but also struck deeply in a culture where sexual degradation is particularly offensive. One blogger, 'Riverbend', wrote that the images were 'like a nightmare come to life':

> Everyone knew this was happening in Abu Ghraib and other places . . . seeing the pictures simply made it all more real and tangible somehow. . . . People are so angry. There's no way to explain the reactions – even pro-occupation Iraqis find themselves silenced by this latest horror. I can't explain how people feel – or even how I personally feel. Somehow, pictures of dead Iraqis are easier to bear than this grotesque show of American military technique. People would rather be dead than sexually abused and degraded by the animals running Abu Ghraib prison. (Riverbend, 2004)

The widespread horror in Iraq and the wider Arab world at the photographs prompted a damage limitation exercise from the White House, including personal apologies by President Bush on some Arab news channels. The images therefore came to be read across the world to some extent in terms of their impact on Arab audiences. This re-reading continued to echo for a long time. One British journalist, writing five months later, described seeing the images 'everywhere in Iraq' – on fliers, on CDs, on videos in the markets and on Iraqi websites. He quoted Sheikh Abdul Sattar Abdul Jabar, the head of the Iraqi

Islamic Clerics Association, saying: 'I have seen a CD show one thousand male and female Iraqis being abused by the Americans. You can watch that CD in the market or you can go to Abu Ghraib and see it with your own eyes' (Fairweather, 2004).

The story of the Abu Ghraib images is not, then, a simple tale of 'digital democratization', but a complex mixture of competition between CBS and the *New Yorker*, of the documentation which surrounded the images, of the particular status of these private digital photographs as insights into the culture within the prison, of the rapid circulation of the images around the world, and of the culture and politics of the Middle East. It also should not be forgotten that, while slow to react, it was elite news outlets that subsequently uncovered much of the abuse story. The *New Yorker*, CBS, *Newsweek* and the *Washington Post* detailed a deliberate lack of clarity in US official policies around the use of torture. European and US newspapers traced the 'extraordinary rendition' of prisoners across Europe and Asia. A number of critics have pointed to the role of some blogs in attempts to shut down journalism which exposed prisoner abuse and torture by US forces. In December 2004, the Associated Press published images found by its reporter Seth Hettena on the commercial image-sharing website Smugmug, showing members of the US Navy's SEAL special forces apparently abusing Iraqi prisoners. The backlash in right-wing and military blogs and other websites against the 'outrageous reporting' of this 'nutbag Islamofascist sympathiser' (Heidt, 2004) almost immediately drowned out questions about prisoner abuse. One newspaper editorial saw the response as typical of a tendency in US public opinion at the time to attack the messenger:

> The Internet echo chamber, predictably, is filled with outrage not at what is depicted in the SEALS photos, but at the reporter who found them and at the newspapers that printed them. Never mind that the photos were apparently available for everyone to see, if they only knew where to look. (*The Virginian-Pilot*, 4 January 2005)

Other journalists received death threats online after producing similarly 'unpatriotic' coverage. Much more insidious for being all the more subtle, however, was the presumption – recurrently reaffirmed across the Western mediascape – that the terms 'abuse' and 'mistreatment' were the most appropriate labels to describe the unconscionable cruelty meted out to Abu Ghraib's prisoners. The concerted efforts of officials to discount the validity of the word 'torture' proved remarkably successful, revealing once again the power and influence institutional authorities wield as news sources in the mainstream press. 'The photos may have driven the story', Bennett et al. point out, 'but the White House communication staff ultimately wrote the captions' (2007: 107).

Our discussion turns in the next section to consider a further example of how imagery taken by an ordinary citizen can decisively unravel the moral tidiness of war, as presented in official accounts, and thereby cast into dispute the legitimacy of official truth claims. 'Leaked from cellphone' was how an anonymous user described a short video they posted on the LiveLeak.com website, the raw footage of which rapidly ignited a blaze of controversy around the globe.

'Too graphic to be suitable'

'Saddam Hussein, the dictator who led Iraq through three decades of brutality, war and bombast before American forces chased him from his capital city and captured him in a filthy pit near his hometown, was hanged just before dawn Saturday during the call to prayer.' With this sentence, the *New York Times* broke the news of Saddam's execution to its readers on 30 December 2006. The front-page news account continues by describing the court process leading up to the hanging, before providing the following details about the actual event, which took place in a former military intelligence building (part of a US base) in northern Baghdad:

> Those in the room said that Mr. Hussein was dressed entirely in black and carrying a Koran and that he was compliant as the noose was draped around his neck.

'He just gave up,' said Mowaffak al-Rubaie, Iraq's national
security adviser. 'We were astonished. It was strange. He just
gave up.'

. . .

Mr. Hussein, in handcuffs, was given to the Iraqis by
American troops. The Iraqis led him from his cell to a judge's
chamber and then to an execution room, a bare unadorned concrete room, according to a witness. It was only a few short steps
up the gallows.

As the rope was placed around his neck, Mr. Hussein turned
to Mr. Rubaie.

'He told me, don't be afraid,' he recounted. 'There was a conversation with him.'

He did not elaborate. He asked that his Koran be given to
someone. Mr. Rubaie took note of the person's name.

Iraqis have Mr. Hussein's body but they have not agreed upon
a place for burial.

As Mr. Hussein awaited the hangman, he was apparently
unaware that the American military was already making plans
to dispose of his personal effects. (Ibid.)

These details, evidently acquired on a second-hand basis by
the newspaper's reporters, appeared to suggest that the Iraqi
government's decision had been implemented in a formal,
methodical and solemn fashion. The description of Saddam,
ostensibly accepting his fate with composure, arguably helped to
reaffirm the impression that the execution proceedings had been
administered dispassionately.

This perception was reinforced, in turn, following the release
within hours of a videotape recording of the execution by Iraqi
government officials. News organizations around the world, in
anticipation that such a videotape would be made available, had
been pondering how best to incorporate it into their coverage.
'I think it might be appropriate at some point to see an image
of Saddam after he is hanged', Steve Capus, president of NBC
News, stated the day before. 'I think about that iconic image
of Nicolae Ceauşescu in Romania, lying literally in the gutter.
I want to do this with a measure of taste, but I don't want to
stand in the way of history' (cited in Carter, 2006). Questions

about matters of taste and propriety, especially in the event that the images proved too graphic to be suitable, were promptly answered by each news organization in turn shortly after two Arab networks, Al Hurra and Al Arabiya, broke the news that Saddam was dead. In the case of BBC News 24, its controller Kevin Bakhurst remarked:

> This morning [30 December 2006] I was in the building as the pictures actually came in from Iraqi television. We showed them on a time delay first on Breakfast to give us the option of cutting out – which we did on first showing.
>
> We quickly reached the decision on Breakfast (and for the early part of the day and evening on BBC One) not to show the noose being put around Saddam's neck as there could be many children on school holiday watching – possibly passively. Even then, we gave a warning ahead of John Simpson's report.
>
> For News 24 and for the late evening bulletin tonight on BBC One, we decided to show all the pictures of the execution as people are choosing actively to watch a news channel – and the late bulletin is on after the watershed [9 pm].
>
> We have also tried to reflect all the voices and views: Shia and Sunni, Arab world, European and American – although no British government minister wants to comment on camera today, nor does President Bush.
>
> I hope the decisions we have made have allowed us to tell the story properly and well across all the channels whilst respecting the audiences they all have, at this time of year in particular. (Bakhurst, 2006)

In the next day's edition of the *New York Times*, John F. Burns (2006) reported that Iraqi citizens had been 'crowding around television sets to watch mesmerizing replays' of the videotape. He explained that it 'showed the 69-year-old Mr. Hussein being led to the gallows at dawn by five masked executioners, and having a noose fashioned from a thick rope of yellow hemp lowered around his neck.' The final portion of the videotape is described as portraying Saddam as appearing 'almost unnaturally calm and cooperative' in his demeanour. 'The message seemed to be that he had lived his final moments with unflinching dignity and

A still from a graphic video of the taunting of Saddam Hussein before his execution by the US-backed Iraqi government, taken with a cellphone camera and distributed on the internet (December 2006). © Rex Features.

courage', Burns wrote, 'reinforcing the legend of himself as the Arab world's strongman that he cultivated while in power.'

Any image of the execution as a duly methodical meting of Iraqi justice would soon be shattered, however, with the startling realization that the execution had been surreptitiously recorded by an observer using a cell phone. The two minutes of grainy, shaky footage – which, unlike the officially authorized video, included an audio track – was widely presumed to have been shot by one of the guards, although the precise circumstances of its production were not revealed. Where the official version had abruptly halted with the tightening of the noose around Saddam's neck, the unofficial version documented his verbal exchanges with his captors (who were clearly determined to torment him), followed by the moment of his demise as the trapdoor opens and drops out of the gallows platform.

The video clip comes to an end with a close-up of Saddam, his neck clearly broken, and the jubilant shouting of several of those gathered in the chamber. In sharp contrast to the 'weirdly calm and dignified' silence of the earlier video, to use the words of the BBC's John Simpson (2006), this version makes readily apparent the extent to which unseen witnesses sought to mock and deride the dictator. 'Altogether, the execution as we now see it is shown to be an ugly, degrading business', Simpson commented, 'which is more reminiscent of a public hanging in the 18th Century than a considered act of 21st Century official justice.' Moreover, he added, the 'most disturbing thing about the new video of Saddam's execution for crimes precisely like this, is that it is all much too reminiscent of what used to happen here.' For Richard B. Woodward (2007), writing in the *Wall Street Journal*, 'in everything from the partisan chants of Shiite bystanders to the grainy, low-lighted jumpiness of the footage and the horror-movie ski masks of the executioners, the video images of the execution contradict the fragile message that a secure and democratic government is in charge, rendering justice to someone who deserves to die.'

The ensuing 'Bluetooth frenzy', as CNN correspondent Arwa Damon labelled it, sparked by the 'snuff reality show', a phrase used by the *New York Times*, attracted considerable attention within the press. An *NYT* editorial published on 4 January 2007 observed that the 'graphic cellphone video' made apparent that the 'condemned dictator appeared to have been delivered from United States military custody into the hands of a Shiite lynch mob.' Among widespread expressions of revulsion, a range of commentators insisted that the footage was likely to inflame sectarian tensions in the region, thereby deepening what was already a desperate crisis. Others concurred, pointing out that Saddam's calmly measured response to his tormentors was certain to generate sympathy in the eyes of some, thereby elevating his status as a martyr. Regarding the attendant media politic, Edward Helmore (2007), writing in London's *The Observer* newspaper, believed the posting of the telephone footage on the internet signalled the end of mainstream news organizations' editorial control over what reaches the public domain. 'This is now a familiar story', he remarked; 'from the savage beheadings of American hostages in Iraq to Saddam's hanging, debate over what should and should not be shown has been made all-but irrelevant in the age of mobile phones and YouTube.' This point was further extended by commentators struck by the ways in which telephone video was evolving into a news tool, one which effectively changed the nature of the news story being reported. 'It brought to a fore the sense that wow, this is a ubiquitous technology', maintained Mark Lukasiewicz, NBC News's vice president for digital media. 'Cameras are now in places where cameras never used to be. That's transformational' (cited by AP, 7 January 2007). The implications of this apparent transformation, whereby digital technology enabled anyone to become an instant news reporter, were profoundly unsettling for some. 'The Saddam video proves again that no act is too gruesome or intimate that someone won't try to take a picture of it and share it with the wired world', Woodward (2007) concluded. 'We better get used to living without visual boundaries – and with the curiosity and flexible morality of the viewer as the only limit on what we can see – from now on.'

'Our digital hall of mirrors'

First-person photography, this analysis of the examples above suggests, renders problematic several familiar assumptions about the mediation of power underpinning visual culture. While the news photograph's claim to offer a literal record – a neutral reflection of reality – is inscribed in the photojournalist's commitment to dispassionate reporting, the image generated by the ordinary citizen makes explicit its interested perspective. Ideology, denied a role in shaping professional form and practice, is reaffirmed as inevitable where interpretation displaces translation. Facts and values converge. The citizen's authority is no more than that of the eyewitness, one whose precarious subjectivity undercuts any rhetorical appeal to the certainties of objectivity, regardless of how comforting the latter may be.

The power of photographs, Susan Sontag argues, is 'to define, not merely record, the most abominable [of] realities' (2003: 21). How she might have assessed the significance of the Saddam Hussein execution video is sadly a matter of speculation, given that she succumbed to leukaemia in December 2004. In her incisive critique of the Abu Ghraib photographs, however, she devoted particular attention to how certain images can 'lay down the tracks' with regard to how conflicts will be judged and remembered. 'Photographs have an insuperable power to determine what we recall of events', she wrote in an essay titled 'Regarding the torture of others', published in May 2004. '[It] now seems probable', she added, 'that the defining associa- tion of people everywhere with the war that the United States launched pre-emptively in Iraq last year will be photographs of the torture of Iraqi prisoners by Americans in the most infamous of Saddam Hussein's prisons, Abu Ghraib.' Photography dis- played its power via this capacity to reveal what was otherwise being denied: specifically, that members of the US military had tortured their prisoners. The meaning of these pictures, she con- tends, involves more than the cruelty of the acts performed: 'the horror of what is shown in the photographs cannot be separated from the horror that the photographs were taken – with the per- petrators posing, gloating, over their helpless captives.' It is this latter dimension which warrants a connection being drawn, in her reading, between these soldiers' casual 'idea of fun' and the 'increasing acceptance of brutality in American life' in everyday contexts. In other words, it follows, it is not sufficient simply to lay the blame on the Bush administration, even though it needs to be recognized that its policies made such acts likely. Rather, it also needs to be acknowledged that these images are representa- tive of the 'fundamental corruptions of any foreign occupation' authorized or condoned by its citizens. 'Considered in this light', she surmises, 'the photographs are us.'

Sontag's intervention, and the fierce backlash it generated from largely pro-war, right-wing commentators, underscores the importance of photography in defining what counts as reality in wartime. And yet, she cautions, such images can do little more than to invite the viewer 'to pay attention, to reflect, to learn, to examine the rationalizations for mass suffering offered by established powers' (2003: 104). Such a careful, methodical contemplation of meaning will likely raise more questions than it will answer, but it is in this difficult commitment to interpretation that insights emerge into how the horrors of war are gradually being normalized as part of our visual culture. Photographs, she reminds us, help to make real matters which we may otherwise choose to ignore, as we struggle to keep other people's pain at a safe distance. In 'our digital hall of mirrors', moral responsibilities cannot be assuaged by official reassurances or justifications. 'The pictures will not go away', Sontag (2004) observes. 'That is the nature of the digital world in which we live.'

This chapter, in endeavouring to examine the capacity of digital images to mediate 'the reality of war', has shown how any such attempt necessarily challenges any journalistic conception of impartiality. Instead, such images, at their best, are socially situated takes from the photographer's perspective, at once provisional and contingent, and, at times, deeply emotive. For many viewers of such images, the honesty of an 'amateur' effort that acknowledges its political stance or commitment is to be valued over and above one which makes a 'professional' appeal to a principle of detachment. Meanwhile the reality of war blurs into multiple realities, some too horrific in their rendering of spectatorship to bear without pain, but still we must look. 'Let the atrocious images haunt us', Sontag (2003) writes. Even if they 'cannot possibly encompass most of the reality to which they refer, they still perform a vital function. The images say: This is what human beings are capable of doing – may volunteer to do, enthusiastically, self-righteously. Don't forget.'

CHAPTER SIX

Making Connections: The Politics of Mediation

Introduction

Declarations of 'cyberwar' reverberated in news headlines in the summer of 2008 as skirmishes between Russia and Georgia threatened to escalate into a fully fledged conflict. Reports relayed accusations that a Russian 'cyber-assault' was under way – said to include the defacement of Georgian government webpages by hackers as well as the waging of dedicated denial of service (DDoS) attacks intended to cripple servers – as tensions between the two countries grew. Precisely who was behind the attacks proved difficult to determine, although it seemed likely it was the work of individual citizens rather than a state-sanctioned intrusion ('the first truly global user-generated conflict', in the words of one commentator). On 8 August, however, the prospect of war suddenly became all too real when Georgia launched a military offensive against South Ossetia, a breakaway region of the country striving for independence. Georgian shelling of Tskhinvali devastated parts of the capital city, with claims emerging about thousands of civilian casualties. Russian troops were rapidly deployed across the border in a counter-attack, one intended to resist the apparent aim of the Georgian government forcibly to incorporate South Ossetia, together with Abkhazia, under direct control. Five days of open conflict between Russian and Georgian forces ensued before an EU peace plan was brokered to produce an agreed ceasefire. Tensions between the countries remain fraught, with Russian officials openly blaming the former Bush administration for deliberately orchestrating the crisis.

Western news coverage was remarkably sparse at its outset.

On the day of Georgia's intervention, press attention was focused primarily on the opening ceremonies of the Beijing Olympics (evidently watched on television by an estimated 1 billion people). News organizations' efforts to secure independent reports from the war zone were typically in vain, with so few journalists being situated anywhere near the outbreak of hostilities. 'Most newspapers hadn't a clue what was going on and lacked sufficient resources to find out', observed Peter Wilby (2008) in *The Guardian*. This when, in 'the age of 24-hour news', the press 'cannot hang about waiting for reporters to arrive', he added. 'Readers want bombs, tanks and death tolls. They need to be told who are the goodies and baddies.' For these and related reasons, initial news reports were long on commentary and speculation, but rather short on concrete facts.

While it is difficult to generalize, much of the mainstream news reporting proceeded to frame the unfolding conflict within the familiar terms of a Cold War binarism, whereby Georgia was characterized as an innocent victim of Russian aggression. In retrospect, it was apparent how few news reports acknowledged that Georgian forces were the first to attack (Georgian President Mikhail Saakashvili proving adept in glossing over this point in news interviews, as well as media savvy enough to employ a Brussels-based PR agency to advance his government's preferred narrative; Paine, 2008). In the US, news organizations encountered a further challenge, namely the risk that comparisons would be drawn with the occupation of Iraq. 'A striking feature of the coverage', the national media watch group FAIR (Fairness & Accuracy In Reporting) pointed out, 'was the ability of pundits who have enthusiastically advocated for US invasions of sovereign countries, dismissing concerns that these would violate international law, to demand that Russia be punished for breaking that same law by violating Georgian sovereignty' (FAIR, 2008). News organizations, in the main, appeared content to overlook this contradiction, preferring instead to reaffirm officially sanctioned perspectives. 'Hypocrisy, unfortunately, was much easier to find in corporate media coverage than disinterested humanitarian concern', FAIR concluded.

Criticisms of the web-based reporting were of a different order. 'Where, in short, were the citizen journalists?' Evgeny Morozov (2008) asked. In expressing his surprise that there were so few eyewitness accounts – in particular, video reports and photographs – available, he called into question the capacity of amateurs to step into the breach in the absence of professional journalists on the scene. Although the range of posts written by both Russian and Georgian bloggers may have been impressive with respect to the spectrum of views on offer, he concedes, the hard news reporting of facts was inadequate. In his words:

> A simple truth about modern conflicts is that they tend to occur in places without universal access to internet broadband and the low ratios of iPhones per capita. It would be sublimely naive – and condescending – to expect South Ossetians or Georgians to respond to intense shellfire by taking a crash-course in podcasting, even if they did have electricity and an internet connection. Tskhinvali and Gori were never going to be hubs of user-generated content from a war-zone.
>
> And yet . . . some 'citizen reports' from Tskhinvali and Gori have emerged despite the technological challenge. This is impressive and welcome, but it comes with a further problem: trust. Most were of poor quality, and many appeared on blogs with no reputation, no previous blogging history (some had been registered only a few days before the war), and carried no identification of a real person with a real name who could claim responsibility for or ownership of them. (Ibid.)

This question of 'trust' is of paramount importance in an 'information war', when each and every claim deserves to be treated with scepticism. The citizen journalist is ill-equipped, Morozov contends, either 'to fill the enormous gaps left by the establishment media' (whose business models call for foreign bureaus to be closed) or to counter the efforts of political leaders seeking to 'take advantage of media blackouts to create narratives favourable to their own political strategies'. Bloggers in the US fared little better, Joshua Foust (2008) suggested in the *Columbia Journalism Review*. While the fighting raged, blogs ordinarily considered to be excellent sources of analysis and insight, in his view, were more often than not 'still linking to the same narrow set of news sources – sources that offered little more than thin quotes from government officials'. In his assessment, the majority of A-list blogs 'retreated to their comfortable and predictable ideological corners', thereby providing sufficient evidence that the blogosphere 'failed to deliver on its original promise: breaking out of the mainstream media's tendency toward groupthink'.

The issues raised in this brief assessment clearly warrant closer scrutiny, but there is every indication that ongoing assessments of the coverage of this crisis provide a useful check against what can be an implicit sense of triumphalism in academic treatments of digital war reporting. While there is undoubtedly enormous potential for content-sharing websites, blogs, cell phones and other media to bring rarely heard voices into the public space, the results may well at times be a restatement of partisan positions to be found in other media or disorganized fragments of experience which do little to disrupt the power of those promoting violent ends to political problems. A simple faith in the ability of the citizen to tell the truth of war founders on the complexities of social life and, of course, on the problem that there is much truth in a range of different perspectives (see also Cottle, 2006, 2009).

In this concluding chapter, we will suggest it is more useful to think of the space of digital media, and particularly the spaces of personal media (such as the cell phone, the digital camera and the content-sharing website), as becoming increasingly politicized during conflict. That is, we must regard citizen media as within, not outside, the politics of war. As states and political groups come to regard these media as potentially powerful, they seek to use them in the conflicts – for example, both Russian and Georgian state media posted partisan news accounts on YouTube (Krikorian, 2008). Individuals used to mediating themselves in digital video or other web-based texts can become caught up in conflict – such as some among the 15,000 young reservists bombed by the Russian military in Gori in the first days of its counter-attack, who posted their own videos online – thereby likely to express their immediate emotions and experiences. In this context, accounts of conflict become part of that conflict to varying degrees. Journalism's traditions of seeking to maintain critical independence from established power are ever more important.

We see evidence of such independence being established in two distinctive ways that contribute to the further development of journalism in digital media – through a radical emphasis upon the individual and through the collecting together and dissemination of knowledge via information networks which disrupt dominance. In the case of the Georgia–South Ossetia conflict, both these trends can be seen in efforts leading to websites such as the Global Voices project, discussed in chapter 4. In their conscious attempts to bridge Eastern and Western perspectives on the conflict, the project's editors linked to (and translated) a range of eyewitness accounts and thoughtful commentaries by citizens from the affected countries. To give one example, its Central and Eastern Europe editor, Veronica Kokhlova, translated into English the blogging of Moscow journalist Ksenia Basilashvili, whose family comes from Tskhinvali. In giving her personal memories of the locality – 'When I hear [Tskhinvali], I imagine the soil warmed up by the sun, a hot lavash [flatbread] right out of the oven, red pungent homemade wine' – Basilashvili refused the competing certainties available on Russian and Western television about who was to blame and who had greater moral authority. She wrote: 'Now it does not matter at all any more. Because while the political and informational wars are taking place, over there – in South Ossetia, in Georgia – people are dying and suffering' (Khokhlova, 2008). When expressed in an individual voice of memory and sorrow, the conflict is irreducibly concerned with human misery, defying any easy purchase of an 'us' or 'them' binarism. In Raymond Williams's (1982) terms, discussed further shortly, the 'culture of distance' by which news media project the horrors of war as remote, seemingly beyond our concern – and thereby reaffirming this type of binarism – cannot be fully sustained while such voices are heard. In addition, the gathering together, translation and dissemination of the individual's testimony by a site such as Global Voices give it both credibility and global reach, making it just a little harder for leaders – in this case presidents Saakashvili, Putin and Bush – or their officials to dominate the information space.

The official story

Assessing the extent to which personal digital media can disrupt ways of seeing war with which publics have become familiar (and therefore shift both elite and public opinion) is central to an understanding of their political role. Such work is beyond the scope of this study, but it can certainly be established that political and military actors talk and act on the understanding that they indeed have that power. In the months leading up to his resignation as British prime minister, Tony Blair gave a series of 'legacy' speeches intended, in part, to help secure his place in the history books on his own preferred terms. In one such speech, delivered on board the assault ship *HMS Albion* on 12 January 2007, he discussed the changing nature of the security challenges facing Western countries in the post-9/11 era. Interestingly, singled out for attention in this regard were the problems posed by 'a completely new world of modern communication and media' for the armed forces. In Blair's words:

> [War] is no longer something read in dispatches. It comes straight into the living room. Take a website like Live Leak which has become popular with soldiers from both sides of the divide in both Afghanistan and Iraq. Operational documentary material, from their mobile phones or laptops, is posted on the site. These sometimes gruesome images are the unmediated reality of war. They provide a new source of evidence for journalists and commentators, by-passing the official accounts and records. (Blair, 2007)

To Blair, such bypassing of official voices weakened the West's war against terrorists, for the pictures, in his estimation, contributed to public reluctance to support long military campaigns.

LiveLeak (www.liveleak.com), whose more controversial content has included images from Abu Ghraib prison deemed too disturbing by news organizations to show, as well as the unedited Saddam Hussein execution clip, is a prominent target of such official attention.

That attention has also included what some see as a veiled threat to make use of these media for political persuasive purposes. The then White House press secretary, Tony Snow (2007), mused, in a briefing to news bloggers the day before Blair's speech, that in the months ahead US soldiers would be using their own cameras to post imagery on these sites so as to show the world what they were really seeing and doing (such footage, Snow insisted, would be more authoritative than that which is typically presented by journalists). For Torcuil Crichton (2007), in the *Sunday Herald*, Blair and Snow were signalling the coalition's determination to open up 'a new propaganda war' by encouraging front-line soldiers to post 'positive video news stories' to counter negative reporting. 'It wouldn't surprise me if governments already do it', Hayden Hewitt, one of the founders of LiveLeak, is quoted as stating. 'There is no quicker way of reaching millions and millions of people than through the internet and, as Tony Blair says, the old ways won't work any more' (cited ibid.).

Underpinning the statements of both government figures and enthusiasts for what Blair called the 'unmediated reality of war' is a belief, then, that these emerging forms of reporting disrupt habitual ways of seeing war, with profound implications for the formation of public opinion. From the perspective of officials, this communicative power is legitimate only to the extent that it respects their definitions of reality. When soldiers' videos or digital snaps bypass proper channels, ending up on such sites as LiveLeak or YouTube, and when civilians or even propagandists for Western governments' enemies post videos of their own on such sites, then control is lost. Indeed, to Blair, control is effectively being handed over to those regarded as terrorists to mediate what counts as reality. In explaining why this must not be allowed to happen, figures such as Blair are effectively forced to acknowledge a politics of mediation that complicates more customary forms of war-fighting rhetoric. The previous chapter's discussion demonstrates why this process of mediation is fraught with ideological tensions, perhaps most powerfully where 'common sense' discourses of patriotism come to bear. The significance of the Abu Ghraib pictures was successfully played down by US officials 'spinning' torture as being little more than the actions of a few 'bad apples'. Similarly, the sudden irruption of the footage of Saddam Hussein's death into the public domain was cast by major news organizations as an editorial debate over questions of 'good taste' where its use was concerned, thereby helping to contain (intentionally or not) its impact on perceptions of the Iraqi government's conduct of the execution. Such efforts on the part of officials to manage the circulation of graphic imagery would appear to have been growing ever since. Access to military-controlled areas of Iraq is increasingly being denied to journalists who refuse to uphold a (largely unspoken) policy forbidding the representation of US combat deaths. Freelance photographer Zoriah Miller, for example, found himself barred from covering the Marines after he posted photos on the internet of three soldiers killed by a suicide bomber (having first waited for their families to be notified). 'It is absolutely censorship', Miller told the *New York Times*. 'I took pictures of something they didn't like, and they removed me. Deciding what I can and cannot document, I don't see a clearer definition of censorship' (cited in Kamber and Arango, 2008). Meanwhile, as the number of casualties on all sides in Iraq escalates, the number of photojournalists there continues to dwindle.

Culture of distance

Part of what is at issue in this politics of mediation is a separation enforced by authorities between the public and the war zone. Bringing the death and misery of war into people's homes by presenting them with images of dead US soldiers, as Miller did, is not just an ethical issue but a political one, for it confronts the public with the profoundly disturbing consequences of war in a way that the images of dead foreigners cannot. In Williams's (1982) terms, war is brought much closer through some forms of representation than others. The televisual tends, in his view, to leave some distance between the viewer and the event, even as it brings that event into the living room.

Writing in the *London Review of Books* at the time of the British military conflict with Argentina over the disputed sovereignty of the Falkland/Malvinas Islands, Williams sought to discern how this 'unnecessary war', to use his apt turn of phrase, was being reported. He argued that underlying the typical sorts of questions that arise when television news reports are examined, such as 'issues of control and independence; of the quality of reporting; of access and balance in discussion', was a deeper problematic. The central technical claim of television, Williams pointed out, is its capacity to represent distant events. While reminding us that the televisual picture of the world is a selective one, he argued that 'what is much more significant is the revealed distance between the technology of television, as professionally understood, managed and interpreted, and the political and cultural space within which it actually operates' (1982: 14).

Across this distance – via the conventions of 'familiar connections' – the tragic devastation endemic to warfare is recurrently taken up and reinflected by television news into an 'antiseptic' representation of reality. Not surprisingly for someone who had experienced conflict first hand, namely as a tank commander in the Second World War, this problem of distance was particularly troubling to Williams, not least in moral terms. Commenting on the daily news reporting of the build-up to the seemingly inevitable outbreak of war on the islands, he wrote:

> After several days of it, feeling the rhythm soaking in, I happened to pass a bonfire of rags and oil in the village and suddenly, in an overwhelming moment, I was in a field in Normandy and the next tank, with my friends in it, was burning and about to explode. I think I then understood the professional culture of distance. (1982: 17)

Of utmost importance, he believed, was the need to understand the ways in which television news shaped the 'representation of spectacular destruction' while, at the same time, serving to 'insulate us from reality' as we watch our television screens in our respective households. Hence the urgency of his call for new investigations to be made into this culture of distance, this 'latent culture of alienation, within which men and women are reduced to models, figures and the quick cry in the throat' (ibid.: 21; see also Williams, [1958] 1989).

As discussed in chapter 3, Western reporting from Afghanistan and Iraq, particularly on television during the invasion phases of both conflicts, undoubtedly replicated this distancing gaze in its coverage. Still more troubling is the fact that this took place with fewer constraints on the journalist than in conflicts such as the 1982 Falklands/Malvinas War or the 1990–1 Gulf War. Journalists were able to roam more freely across the battlefield and report live, both because of new mobile technologies and on account of the US military's embedding policy. They also operated within a political space broadened by calls from dissenting voices among governments and opinion leaders that resolving conflict requires 'dialogue and respect for the other' (de Villepin, 2003). Yet journalism did little to challenge the antiseptic spectacle. In Kaldor's (2006) description of 'spectacle war', high-tech journalism became a tool of warfare itself as its live coverage of events such as the 'shock and awe' bombing of Baghdad on 21 March 2003 sent messages of American power to both US and Iraqi audiences. To Virilio (1989, 1994), and critics who have drawn on his work, the media's pursuit of speed, as communications technologies improve, has had the effect of reducing the distance between the military's rifle sight and the journalist's lens, while increasing the distance between journalism and the human targets of war. Within a discourse which privileges the immediacy of the live image, there appears to be simply no time to see afresh. Jingoistic media, particularly in the US, presented audiences with enormous quantities of images from battle, including the staged 'saving' of Private Jessica Lynch from an

Iraqi hospital and the toppling of the statue of Saddam Hussein in Firdos Square, Baghdad, in ways set in motion by military public relations.

To some, the 2003 invasion of Iraq therefore represented the final stages in a crisis in war reporting. Knightley (2004) contended pessimistically that Western journalists were being thrown back into a dependent relationship on those who wage wars. Looking back on reporting of the invasion, he saw a loss of autonomy and consequently of the moral authority of journalists as witnesses to conflict: 'The age of the war correspondent as hero is clearly over. Whether they wish to continue as propagandists and myth makers, subservient to those who wage the wars, is a decision they will have to take themselves' (Knightley, 2004: 548). More recently, former BBC war correspondent Martin Bell has expressed his own deep misgivings, even going so far as to contend that the 'honourable profession' of war reporting 'has been laid to rest'. Journalists, he argues, have ceased to be 'peripheral observers' (in the tradition of William Howard Russell covering the Crimea in the mid-1850s), becoming instead 'influential players in the theatre of war'. 'Today's war reporters operate in the frenzy of the rolling news cycle with the pressure on them to be the first and fastest rather than the most reliable', he observes. '[T]he proliferating rolling news channels show more than they know, and what they know is usually very little at the time when they go to air: *Never wrong for long* should be their watchword' (Bell, 2008: 222). Much like war itself, Bell maintains, war reporting has been so dramatically transformed that previous understandings of it have ceased to be relevant. The wars in Afghanistan and Iraq, he believes, are being fought on a media landscape that makes independent, free-ranging news gathering all but impossible. The Pentagon, in particular, is singled out for deliberately targeting news outlets, whether they are Western journalists (he cites the British ITN reporter Terry Lloyd 'blown away by US Marines', for example) or Arab satellite channels such as Al Jazeera or Al Arabiya. 'The wars of the 21st century offer no immunity to anyone not carrying a gun', Bell insists.

Confronted with these types of dangers, Bell contends that television news has retreated from the 'real world', favouring instead the 'reporter-as-celebrity' who practises 'rooftop journalism' in relative safety far from the battlefield. Its obsession with 'froth and fluff' underscores the extent to which it has lost its nerve – the '"stupidification" of its agenda' being directly tied to financial imperatives whereby profit is prioritized over public service. In this climate, it is not surprising that television imposes censorship upon itself, which in Bell's view has little to do with operational security. Rather, it has everything to do with ensuring that viewers are not distressed by images of real-world violence. Drawing upon his own experience, Bell recalls:

> I fought this battle with my editors, and lost it, throughout the Balkan wars of the 1990s. We were allowed to show the Croat militia blazing away with their Kalashnikovs, the JNA artillery pounding Vukovar with old American Howitzers, the Muslims fiercely defending their parts of Sarajevo. But in every case we showed the outgoing fire, and not nearly enough of the effects of the incoming: the death and destruction, the bloodshed and horror, the waste of young lives, even in some cases the grieving of relatives, because that would be too upsetting.

The consequences, he continues, are far-reaching:

> We were not just prettifying war, we were falsifying it. And this is dangerous, because if you obscure the reality it then becomes an acceptable way of settling differences. No wonder this generation of peacetime politicians resorts to it so easily. (2008: 230–1)

It is on these grounds, then, that Bell advances his thesis – not without personal pain – that war reporters of his generation 'have failed in our most basic of tasks – to tell the truth about warfare'. Good taste censorship, as he calls it, is simply unacceptable.

Knightley calls for a return to the 'truthful, objective and balanced reporting that good correspondents once did their best to provide' (Knightley, 2004: 525). Yet it is a plea which his authoritative account of Western war reporting itself undercuts, for he finds little evidence that war reporting has ever achieved these goals. Bell's response, and that of other prominent war reporters such as Robert Fisk, has been to espouse a journalism that is committed to the underdog or the victim (see Bell, 1998; Fisk, 2008). Without digressing into the large literature on the role of objectivity within journalism, it is sufficient to say here that the exploration of digital reporting in this book provides evidence that other modes of independent journalism are being made increasing use of by journalists facing the multiple challenges of reporting contemporary war outlined by Knightley and Bell. In particular, we have highlighted modes of representing war in which the professionalized distance of the objective reporter has given way to much more personal forms of reporting. These range from the personal e-mails of Baghdad correspondent Farnaz Fassihi in October 2004 about the impossibility of reporting safely or adequately any more, which brought home to US readers the collapse of order in the city, to the poignant blog entries from citizens of Yangon, Burma, in September 2007, about the sudden extreme danger of walking in the streets outside their houses. The personal authority of the subjective account has the potential, in certain circumstances, both to cut through the myth-making which Knightley decries and to close the 'antiseptic' distance which Williams fears in televisual representations of war.

The personal voice as independent

We began the book with a discussion of Kevin Sites's attempts to report the execution of wounded fighters in Falluja by a US Marine, attempts thwarted by 'good taste censorship' at NBC but which he could personally articulate on his own blog. In light of the discussion above, however, perhaps the greater lesson from the Sites story is not so much the use of the internet to present truths abut the horrors of war but rather its use to present the experience of being in that horror. As Sites reflected later in a video interview, his blog allowed him to explain his own understanding of what witnessing and recording those events meant:

It allowed me to provide a personal viewpoint of what was going on, how I was feeling while I was covering these things, that I normally wouldn't do in an NBC report, plus it allowed me to explain the role of my profession as a journalist, what we're supposed to do, another thing you wouldn't do in a straightforward report. And I was able to do all those things and I think it clarified for a lot of people what had actually happened there. It created this sense of understanding that had not come across in the story that we reported for NBC. And it made it clear to me at that point really the power of the Internet . . . I felt like this potentially saved my career. It allowed me to tell the story I hadn't told on the network news. (Wired, 2008)

The intense pressures negotiated by those caught up in the morally difficult terrain of war experience over what is usually reported becomes visible at such moments. At such moments, too, the distancing of war is perhaps lessened. If television is at risk of representing distant events as 'over there', digital reporting tools, in which the individual correspondent comes to the forefront of the act of communication, have some potential to represent people in distant and sometimes unimaginable situations simply as individuals, and therefore open up possibilities of empathy and fellow feeling. Thus Katz (2003: ix) wrote, in his summary of the impact of Salam Pax's ground-breaking blog, in which distant political decisions to bomb or cut off Baghdad translate as residents' struggles to live as the cost of water and bread spirals: 'He was just like us' (see also Griffiths, 2003).

At the same time as more subjective modes of reporting war have grown in status, the status of the journalist as external observer to war has weakened. Whether because of a post-Vietnam distrust between journalists and the military, or a greater emphasis by authorities on the management of the media, or journalism's loss of authority in wider culture, or indeed the growing power of the media as a platform of social life, there is no doubt that the notion of journalists as neutral witnesses has become less tenable. As detailed in earlier chapters, the greater management of journalists has been accompanied by a loss of protection for reporters, resulting in a rapidly rising death rate.

Since the September 11 attacks – spectacular acts of symbolically charged violence – the perception of media as part of conflict has intensified. Seib (2003: 632) noted that, of the thirty-three groups designated as 'terrorist' by the US government, nineteen had websites at the time he was writing. The US government, for its part, started its $60 million-a-year Al Hurra Arabic-language news channel as a response. Discourses of freedom and of self-determination are invoked by all sides to justify the launch of these media, putting any space of neutral reporting under severe pressure. As Mohammed Afif, news director of the Hizbollah-sponsored Al Manar television station, commented:

> It's very difficult to separate between the cause and the work. Anyway, I would ask you, do you know any neutral media in the world. Can we say the BBC, for instance, is neutral, is CNN neutral . . . Are we soldiers, yes, maybe, but are we first professional journalists. (PBS, 2007)

Al Manar is indeed regarded by Israel as all but a combatant, and its offices were repeatedly bombed by Israel during the 2007 Lebanese War. News organizations which seek a position of independence from politics fare little better. Al Jazeera's offices in both Kabul and Baghdad were bombed by the US military, a sign for some that reporting that is too independent is unacceptable to governments. The power of news images of death and misery from conflicts is certainly a target of criticism from those seeking to make war appear a solution to political problems, as shown by Blair's comments cited earlier.

In this context of an intensified politicization of the space of professional news, the voice of the individual has leapt to the fore in such forms as the independent journalist's blog or video report, the 'accidental journalism' of citizens and participants whose personal media become shared publicly. All these make sense, to a greater or lesser degree, in terms of a discourse of integrity. In this discourse, what is lost in authority, as the writing takes place without institutional support, is understood to be gained in credibility. Reporters such as Chris

Allbritton, who travelled to northern Iraq in 2003 through donations by readers of his blog, could claim to reconvene their audiences in a space that was to an extent outside this fraught politics. Vaughan Smith, the freelancer who reported on UK troops in Afghanistan's Helmand province in 2007, found that the digital media of the blog and the hand-held video camera gave him an independence from editors and managers he had never experienced before. 'In Helmand I worked to fill my own weblog and, for the first time, I was solely responsible for my own work' (Smith, 2007). The end result of editing and producing his work online was a rawer journalism, in which cutaways, voiceovers and other techniques were discarded in favour of long use of interviewees. As we have noted elsewhere (Matheson and Allan, 2007), this impressionistic journalism connotes to many an absence of mediation and therefore greater veracity.

More importantly, the simplification of journalism to an individual communicating to her or his readers reintroduces the interpersonal. Joshua Kucera, discussed in chapter 3, was not alone in being 'blown away' by the extent to which a genuine relationship was experienced with readers who cared for him and entered into discussion with him. The power of eyewitness testimony from inhabitants of Beirut under attack from Israeli missiles or from inhabitants of Gori, Georgia, occupied by Russian troops, lies not so much in what is seen as in the connection established between individuals entangled in war and those reading their blogs or watching their online videos. In a different kind of interpersonal connection, many viewers of the Abu Ghraib images – judging from reactions expressed in places such as the blogosphere – felt profoundly upset by the inhumanity of the individual soldiers and military contractors who took them. In Richard Rorty's terms, these media invite audiences to be 'partisans of solidarity', imaginatively identifying with the details of others' lives as part of the process of understanding the events in which they are situated (1991: 29; see also Ettema and Glasser, 1998: 200).

Journalism of connections

The changing nature of war has undoubtedly altered the way in which media are implicated. No longer simply propaganda tools to mobilize enlistment and public support, media are central to both the strategies and the more immediate tactics of information warfare. In a number of earlier chapters, the centrality of personal digital media in contemporary conflict, from cell phones to the individual use of image-sharing sites, has been highlighted. From Kevin Sites's reassertion – and reinterpretation – of his journalistic task on his personal website to John Sloboda's avowedly amateur witnessing of civilian casualty figures on Iraq Body Count, the force behind the challenge to political orthodoxy is intertwined with personal media's emphasis upon individual selfhood. The expression of common humanity by individuals caught up in war or observing from the sidelines carries particular weight in this context.

Yet the fragmented and opinionated spaces of the blogosphere raise fears in many quarters about quality, particularly given the large claims made for the blog's mixture of the intensely personal voice and the public uses to which it is sometimes put. As discussed in chapter 4, there are concerns that blogs are frequently low on information, that they contain often vituperative attacks on others, that they isolate people within communities of like-minded individuals. Cohen (2006) notes that blogs can be accused of being at once too public, in their display of what is usually private, and not public enough, in their focus upon the self. There is much to these criticisms, and the points can be extended also to related media such as content-sharing or community-forming sites. The disappointment of observers of the Georgian and Russian blogospheres can be matched elsewhere. Haas (2005), for example, surveys a number of studies which suggest warblogs that emerged in the US after the 2001 attacks often reflected broadcast and print news sources, contributing little that was new. The fury of attacks in some right-wing blog networks on journalists who were regarded as biased, including former CNN chief news executive Eason Jordan or Associated Press photographer Bilal Hussein (see chapter 4), fell short of good quality journalism by almost any standard. In stark contrast, where citizen media have been more organized, around either institutional political objectives or editorial norms, the way they work has often been quite different, with distinct implications for the knowledge that emerges. This is true of networks that seek to constrain their members, such as the (probably) state-organized Official Community of Saudi Bloggers, whose members agree not to criticize the country's royal family, government policies or religious authorities (Hammond, 2006). It is also, however, true of networks that seek to provide a stage on which information and political activism against powerful interests can flourish.

Among the latter category is the website of the Sokwanele Civic Action Support Network ('sokwanele' translates from the Shona as 'enough is enough'), an organization committed to undermining the Zimbabwean ZANU-PF government of Robert Mugabe through peaceful means. Like the Burmese networks discussed in chapter 4, Sokwanele.com is part of a sophisticated information network of political exiles and underground activists, who ensure information about abuses of political freedoms and other human rights is shared and used to support change. The Sokwanele site appeared to begin as a newsletter in 2007 aimed at an international audience. It drew on cell-phone networks among activists who shared information about political violence and resistance, much as *samizdat* publications had done in Eastern Europe and the Soviet Union during the Cold War. As one of its anonymous writers commented, 'talking about a revolution looks like an SMS message' in Zimbabwe (Sokwanele, 2007). The site was used in March 2008 as a gathering point for presidential and parliamentary election results, sent in by activists through cell-phone pictures taken of the numbers posted outside polling stations across Zimbabwe. Mugabe's loss in the first round of the presidential vote can be attributed in part to this networked citizen monitoring of the count, which made vote-rigging by government officials more difficult. At the same time the site launched a 'mash-up', or combination of media, comprising an interactive Google map of Zimbabwe overlaid with instances of breaches of fair electoral process, from intimidation and beatings to the removal of individuals from the electoral roll. This feature soon grew into a testament to the crackdown in the build-up to the presidential run-off poll, and by September 2008 showed more than 2,100 instances of political abuse. The site soon hosted images of the political violence as well, gathered again from supporters across the country, and increasingly outspoken, though anonymous, bloggers.

Sokwanele's position in the country appears complex. It is most likely funded by Western governments or businesses with an interest in regime change, although this is unclear, and its links with other political groups in the country are also hazy (Dixon, 2008). Its purpose appears to be a thorn in the side of the government through information, distributed as fliers, audio tapes, text messages and web-based material. What is apparent, however, is that the near real-time distribution of information on the site, its tally of abuses and the voices of dissent it amplifies belong to a networked form of citizen power with considerable power in a country where state control of the media is high. This is a symbolic power, an expression of a collective refusal to accept ZANU-PF's oppression. It does not appear to be so much a form of media power which precipitates or facilitates action, such as Rheingold (2002) perceived in mobile media such as cell-phone texting during recent changes in political power in the Philippines. To begin with, few in Zimbabwe have regular access to the internet. Nor is Sokwanele's such power primarily that of informing or convening audiences, such as real-time media possess in letting viewers see conflict taking place live in distant places. For the website and cell-phone network are immediate more in the sense of providing a platform on which politics may take place, in the linking up of moments of pain and death into a meaningful picture of resistance. While perhaps not a model for public communication elsewhere, as its approach and meaning are embedded in the Zimbabwean context, it provides evidence of the way the aggregation of information and often harrowing personal stories gathered through the micro-media of cell phones and e-mail can form powerful public texts of a distinct kind. Unlike the Belgrade radio station B92, whose editors were surprised at the listenership of people outside the country, Sokwanele appears to have an explicit double orientation – to the people of Zimbabwe, in order to build resistance, and to the outside world, as a witness of the political violence taking place. The internet's indiscriminate distribution can be used to issue an invitation to the wider world to acknowledge political struggle within the country. Or, to put it another way, the internet is used to wage resistance against ZANU-PF on a global stage which the opposition has itself built. Significantly, this recognition of the power of the internet is accompanied not by a claim to be independent, balanced journalism, as was the case with B92, but by partisan, individualized voices.

Final thoughts

To close, it is readily apparent that what counts as digital war reporting is in a state of flux, with familiar principles being recast anew by competing imperatives of convergence in the mainstream media – and by those of divergence being played out in the margins by 'the people formerly known as the audience', to use blogger Jay Rosen's (2006) apt turn of phrase. In the final weeks of writing this book, the journalistic potential – as well as the possible risks – of social networking, for example, have been made readily apparent. During the hostage crisis in Mumbai in November 2008, the role played by ordinary citizens using the micro-blogging service Twitter feeds to relay vital insights attracted extensive comment.

Time and again, Twitter was singled out for praise as the best source for real-time citizen news. Even before news of the attacks had appeared in the electronic media, it was providing eyewitness accounts from users describing what was happening in the best way they could manage under the circumstances. Examples of messages or 'tweets' (posts being limited to 140 characters), some of which were cited in various news reports, included the following:

> One terrorist has jumped from Nariman house building to Chabad house – group of police commandos have arrived on scene. (Anonymous, #mumbai channel)

> Special anti-hijacking group called Rangers entering Nariman House, at least 80 commandos. (scorpfromhell)

> Hospital update. Shots still being fired. Also Metro cinema next door. (mumbaiattack)

> Blood needed at JJ hospital. (aeropolowoman)

> Fascinating. CNN is filling airtime; #mumbai channel is full of tidbits posted by witnesses. (yelvington)

> At least 80 dead, 250 injured. American and British targeted. (ArtVega)

Saad Khan (2008), at the Green & White blog, described a 'Tweets frenzy' where 'minute-by-minute updates about the location of the blasts/skirmishes, positions of the security forces, location of the journalists and safe passages for stranded commuters', among other topics, were shared. In the hours that followed, the majority of tweets were relaying secondary observations taken from mainstream news reports, correcting previous messages, or offering links to online sources for fresh perspectives. Examples of the last were links to sites such as a Google map, which documented the location of the attacks, as well as Wikipedia and Mahalo, which constantly updated known facts. Videos in the dozens were being uploaded to YouTube, while Flickr displayed users' photographs ('Vinu' posting particularly grisly images). Sites such as Metblogs Mumbai, GroundReport, Global Voices, NowPublic, Poynter.org, and iReport.com, among countless others, were busy aggregating citizen reports. Meanwhile major news organizations, such as BBC News, were moving swiftly to gather insights. NYTimes.com asked its readers in the city to e-mail photographs or to insert a written description of events in the 'comment field' on its webpage. In the hours and days to follow, however, it was Twitter that won plaudits for capturing the rawness of the tragedy in reportorial terms. 'Last night', Claudine Beaumont of the *Daily Telegraph* pointed out, 'the social web came of age' (*Daily Telegraph*, 27 November 2008). Stephanie Busari (2008) of CNN agreed: 'It was the day social media appeared to come of age and signaled itself as a news-gathering force to be reckoned with.' This was not to deny its limitations as a trustworthy news source – serious criticisms having surfaced about inaccuracies and rumours being circulated – but rather to acknowledge the potential of social networking for first-hand crisis news, and thereby an important dimension to digital war reporting.

This book has taken as its focus some of the ways in which digital war reporting opens up alternative spaces for acts of witnessing across a range of platforms. Various forms and practices have been shown to throw into sharp relief the narrow ideological parameters within which mainstream news media typically operate. Journalists' routine, everyday choices about what to report – how best to do it, and why – necessarily implicate them in a discursive politics of mediation. The very multi-vocality at the heart of their narrativization of reality renders problematic any one claim to truth, and in so doing reveals that witnessing is socially situated, perspectival and thus politicized. Before digital war reporting can become interactively dialogical in any meaningful sense of the term, however, it will have to counter the forms of social exclusion endemic to the culture of distance. A first step in this direction, as this book has sought to demonstrate, is to recognize that the culture of distance is, simultaneously, a culture of othering. At stake, in our view, is the need to deconstruct journalism's 'us and them' dichotomies precisely as they are taken up and reinflected in news accounts where the structural interests of 'people like us' are counterpoised against the suffering of strangers. To recast the imperatives of 'here' and 'there', and thereby resist the familiar pull of the culture of distance, it is the corresponding gap between knowledge and action that will have to be overcome.

References

Abdulhamid, A. (2006) Just the facts: Truth and the Internet. *OpenDemocracy*, 14 June. Available at http://www.opendemocracy.net/arts-Literature/pen4_3643.jsp.

Agence France Presse (2004) Iraq's secret daily death toll: No one knows the true price of the violence. 11 July.

Agrell, S. (2005) Military postings: Forces struggle to control information leaks. *National Post*, 27 August, A1.

Ahluwalia, P. (2006) Delivering freedom: Australia's witnessing of Abu Ghraib. *Journal of Visual Culture*, 5, 93–6.

Al Arji, F. (2006) An Iraqi blogger to America: You're living a lie. *Daily Star* [Beirut], 31 May.

Al Hussaini, A. (2006) Arabisc: Sexual harassment and the Egyptian blogosphere. *Global Voices Online*, 30 October. Available at http://www.globalvoicesonline.org/2006/10/30/arabisc-sexual-harrassment-and-the-egyptian-blogosphere/ [sic].

Al Jazeera (2003) Al Jazeera correspondent killed in US attack. *Al Jazeera News*, 8 April. Available at http://globalresearch.ca/articles/ALJ304B.html.

Allan, S. (2006) *Online news: Journalism and the Internet*. Maidenhead: Open University Press.

Allan, S., and Thorsen, E. (eds) (2009) *Citizen journalism: Global perspectives*. New York: Peter Lang.

Allan, S., and Zelizer, B. (eds) (2004) *Reporting war: Journalism in wartime*. London: Routledge.

Allbritton, C. (2003) Blogging from Iraq. *Nieman Reports*, 57 (3), 82–4. Available at http://www.nieman.harvard.edu/reports/03-3NRfall/V57N3.pdf.

Allemang, J. (2003) Where everybody is a war reporter. *Toronto Globe and Mail*, 29 March, F3.

Andén-Papadopoulos, K. (2008) The Abu Ghraib torture photographs. *Journalism*, 9 (1), 5–30.

Andersen, R. (2006) *A century of media, a century of war*. New York: Peter Lang.

Andrews, P. (2003) Is blogging journalism? *Nieman Reports*, 57 (3), 63–4.

Armitage, J. (1999) Paul Virilio: An introduction. *Theory, Culture and Society*, 16 (5–6), 1–23.

Arnett, P. (1998) Goodbye, world. *American Journalism Review*, November.

Artz, L., and Kamalipour, Y. R. (2005) *Bring 'em on: Media and politics in the US war on Iraq*. Lanham, MD: Rowman & Littlefield.

Au, W. J. (2004) Silence of the blogs. *Salon.com*, 23 January. Available at http://archive.salon.com/tech/feature/2004/01/23/baghdad_gamer_two/index.html.

Bakhurst, K. (2006) Saddam's execution. *The Editors* blog, BBC, 30 December. Available at http://www.bbc.co.uk/blogs/theeditors/2006/12.

Barber, N. (1999) Battling on home front to get the story out. *The Scotsman*, 2 April.

Bardoel, J. (1996) Beyond journalism: A profession between information society and civil society. *European Journal of Communication*, 11 (3), 283–302.

Barringer, F. (1999) A new war drew new methods for covering it. *New York Times*, 21 June.

Bauman, Z. (2000) *Liquid modernity*. Cambridge: Polity.

BBC (2001) John Simpson: Action addict. BBC News, 17 November. Available at http://news.bbc.co.uk/2/hi/in_depth/uk/2000/newsmakers/1660087.stm.

BBC (2003) Minutes of editorial policy meeting. BBC, 6 May. Available at http://www.bbc.co.uk/guidelines/editorialguidelines/assets/meetings/may2003minutes.doc.

BBC (2006) Interview transcript: John Sloboda. Newsnight, 28 April. Available at http://news.bbc.co.uk/2/hi/programmes/newsnight/4950254.stm.

Beckerman, G. (2007) The new Arab conversation. *Columbia Journalism Review*, 45 (5), 16–23.

Bell, M. (1995) *In harm's way*. London: Penguin.

Bell, M. (1998) The journalism of attachment. In M. Kieran (ed.), *Media ethics*. London, Routledge, pp. 15–22.

Bell, M. (2003) Media: Say no to news on tap. *The Independent*, 16 December, 8.

Bell, M. (2008) The death of news. *Media, War & Conflict*, 1 (2), 221–31.

Bennahum, D. S. (1997) The Internet revolution. *Wired*, April.

Bennett, W. L. (2003) Communicating global activism. *Information, Communication and Society*, 6 (2), 143–168.

Bennett, W. L., Lawrence, R. G., and Livingston, S. (2007) *When the press fails: Political power and the news media from Iraq to Katrina*. Chicago: University of Chicago Press.

Berenger, R. D. (2004) *Global media go to war: Role of news and entertainment media during the 2003 Iraq war*. Spokane, WA: Marquette Books.

Berenger, R. D. (2006) Introduction: War in cyberspace. *Journal of Computer-Mediated Communication*, 12 (1). Available at http://jcmc.indiana.edu/vol12/issue1/berenger.html.

Bernton, H. (2004) The somber task of honoring the fallen. *Seattle Times*, 18 April.

Biggs, B. S. (1999) Truth be told? *San Francisco Bay Guardian*, 12 April.

Blair, T. (2007) Transcript: Prime Minister Tony Blair speaks at RUSI. Rusi.org, 11 January. Available at http://www.rusi.org/events/ref:E45A6104E7E1A8/info:public/infoID:E45A611EFEA3F2/.

Boczkowski, P. J. (2004) *Digitizing the news: Innovation in online newspapers*. Cambridge, MA: MIT Press.

Boese, C. (2004) The spirit of Paolo Freire in blogland: Struggling for a knowledge-log revolution. *Into the blogosphere: Rhetoric, community and culture of weblogs*, Available at http://blog.lib.umn.edu/blogosphere/the_spirit_of_paulo_freire.html.

Boyer, P. J. (2003) The new war machine: A reporter at large. *New Yorker*, 79, 30 June.

Bruns, A. (2008) Gatewatching, gatecrashing: Futures for tactical news media. In M. Boler (ed.), *Digital media and democracy: Tactics in hard times*. Cambridge, MA: MIT Press, pp. 247–70.

Burns, J. F. (2006) Hussein video grips Iraq: Attacks go on. *New York Times*, 31 December.

Busari, S. (2008) Tweeting the terror: How social media reacted to Mumbai. CNN, 27 November.

BusinessWire (2001) CBS uses Viewpoint technology in 'America fights back' photos on web site. *BusinessWire*, 26 October. Available at Factiva database, bwr0000020011025dxapooh4x.

Caldwell, C. (1999) wwwar.reporting. *American Spectator*, September.

Campbell, A. (1999) Communications lessons for NATO, the military and media. Speech to the Royal United Services Institute for Defence Studies. *RUSI Journal*, 1 August.

Campbell, K. (2001) Today's war reporting: It's digital, but dangerous. *Christian Science Monitor*, 4 December, 2.

Carter, B. (2006) How much should be shown of a hanging? Network executives wonder and wait. *New York Times*, 30 December.

Castells, M. (2000) *The rise of the network society*. 2nd edn, Oxford: Blackwell.

Castells, M. (2001) *The Internet galaxy: Reflections on the Internet, business, and society*. Oxford: Oxford University Press.

CJR (Columbia Journalism Review) (2006) Into the abyss: Reporting Iraq 2003–2006: An oral history. *Columbia Journalism Review*, 45 (4).

Cohen, K. R. (2006) A welcome for blogs. *Continuum*, 20 (2), 161–73.

Conetta, C. (2002) Operation Enduring Freedom: Why a higher rate of civilian bombing casualties. Project on Defense Alternatives, *Briefing Report #13*, 24 January. Available at http://www.comw.org/pda/02010ef.html.

Cottle, S. (2006) *Mediatized conflict*. Maidenhead and New York: Open University Press.

Cottle, S. (2009) *Global crisis reporting*. Maidenhead and New York: Open University Press.

CPJ (Committee to Protect Journalists) (n.d.) Journalists killed in 2003: 42 confirmed. Committee to Protect Journalists: Defending journalists wordwide. Available at http://www.cpj.org/deadly/2003_list.html.

Cramer, C. (2004) Keynote address. Fujitsu Siemens Computers VISIT 2004 conference, 7 October.

Crandall, J. (2005) Operational Media. *ctheory*, 1 June. Available at http://www.ctheory.net/articles.aspx?id=441.

Crawley, J. W. (1999) Net hums with news about war. Copley News Service, 30 March.

Crichton, T. (2007) Blair and Bush's latest weapon of war: YouTube. *Sunday Herald*, 14 January.

Cumings, B. (1992) *War and television*. London: Verso.

Danner, M. (2004) Abu Ghraib: The hidden story. *New York Review of Books*, 51, 7 October. Available at http://www.nybooks.com/articles/article-preview?article_id=17430.

Dao, J., and Lichtblau, E. (2004) The struggle for Iraq: The images. Soldier's family set in motion chain of events on disclosure. *New York Times*, 3 August. Available at http://query.nytimes.com/gst/fullpage.html?res=9B01E4D9143CF93BA35756C0A9629C8B63.

Deborah Norville Tonight (2004) Worth a thousand words. MSNBC TV, 13 May. Available at http://www.msnbc.msn.com/id/4964024/.

Debrix, F. (2007) *Tabloid terror: War, culture, and geopolitics*. New York: Routledge.

Deibert, R. J. (2008) Black code redux: Censorship, surveillance, and the militarization of cyberspace. In M. Boler (ed.), *Digital media and democracy: Tactics in hard times*. Cambridge, MA: MIT Press, 137–63.

Der Derian, J. (2001) *Virtuous war: Mapping the military–industrial–media–entertainment network*. Boulder, CO: Westview Press.

Der Derian, J. (2004) James Der Derian on imagining peace. Transcript of interview, Massive Change Radio, Available at http://www.massivechange.com/media/MIL_JamesDerDerian.pdf.

Deuze, M. (2005) Towards professional participatory storytelling in journalism and advertising. *firstmonday*, 10 (7). Available at http://www.firstmonday.org/issues/issue10_7/index.html.

Dixon, R. (2008) Zimbabwe's split opposition. *Los Angeles Times*, 8 July, A4.

Dodge, T. (2003) An Iraqi in cyberspace. *Times Literary Supplement*, 24 October, 27.

Dowell, W. T. (2005) Mediators and the media. Oslo forum 2005: Background papers, Available at http://www.osloforum.org/datastore/ Mediators%20Retreats/Retreat%20Website/Mediatorsandmedia.pdf.

Ehrlich, R. S. (2007) Myanmar's blogs of bloodshed. *Asian Times Online*, 29 September. Available at http://www.atimes.com/atimes/Southeast_ Asia/II29Ae02.html.

El-Nawawy, M., and Iskander, A. (2003) *Al-Jazeera: The story of the network that is rattling governments and redefining modern journalism.* Boulder, CO: Westview Press.

Ettema, J. S., and Glasser, T. L. (1998) *Custodians of conscience: Investigative journalism and public virtue.* New York: Columbia University Press.

FAIR (2008) Georgia/Russia conflict forced into Cold War frame. FAIR. org, 14 August. Available at http://www.fair.org/index.php?page=3596.

Fairweather, J. (2004) Abuse propaganda fuels the hatred of westerners. *Daily Telegraph*, 21 September. Available at http://www.telegraph.co.uk/ news/main.jhtml?xml=/news/2004/09/22/wirq322.xml.

Fancher, M. (2004a) Powerful photograph offered chance to tell an important story. *Seattle Times*, 18 April.

Fancher, M. (2004b) Worldwide interest in coffins photo was surprising, gratifying. *Seattle Times*, 2 May.

Feldman, C. (2006) Haditha: Is McGirk the new Mary Mapes? *American Thinker*, 9 June. Available at http://www.americanthinker. com/2006/06/haditha_is_mcgirk_the_new_mary.html.

Feuilherade, P. (2004) Reporting Falluja: 'America's second war' in Iraq. Text of editorial analysis, BBC Monitoring Service. International News Safety Institute, 9 November. Available at http://www.newssafety.com/ stories/bbc/iraq9.htm.

Filkins, D. (2003) Muted joy as troops capture an Iraqi town. *New York Times*, 22 March, 1.

Fisk, R. (2008) *The age of the warrior: Selected essays.* New York: Nation Books.

Flournoy, E. (2003) Satellite newsgathering crosses the digital divide. *Online Journal of Space Communication*, 5. Available at http://satjournal. tcom.ohiou.edu/Issue5/cur_media.html.

Flynn, A. (1999) War in cyberspace the real thing. Canadian Press Newswire, 14 April.

Foerstel, H. N. (2006) *Killing the messenger: Journalists at risk in modern warfare.* Westport, CT: Praeger.

Foust, J. (2008) How blogging failed the war in Georgia. *Columbia Journalism Review*, 19 August.

Franklin, H. B. (1994) From realism to virtual reality: Images of America's wars. In S. Jeffords and L. Rabinovitz (eds), *Seeing through the media*. New Brunswick, NJ: Rutgers University Press.

Frey, J. (1999) 'Subject: we are all in danger': In e-mail from Kosovo, a terrifying message. *Washington Post*, 29 March.

Friedman, D. (2006) Postcards from hell. *Australian Magazine*, 10 June, 21.

Friend, C., and Singer, J. B. (eds) (2007) *Online journalism ethics*. Armonk, NY: M. E. Sharpe.

Galber, N. (2002) Seeking perspective on the movie front lines. *New York Times*, 27 January, 4.

Gandhi (2005) Iraq the model: The full story. *Bush Out*, 25 January. Available at http://bushout.blogspot.com/2005/01/iraq-model-full-story-i-was-busy.html.

Gandhi (2007) Bush cites Fadhils for proof of 'success' in Iraq! *Bush Out*, 29 March. Available at http://bushout.blogspot.com/2007/03/omfg-bush-cites-fadhils-for-proof-of.html.

Gans, H. J. (1980) *Deciding what's news: A study of CBS evening news, NBC nightly news, Newsweek, and Time*. New York: Vintage Books.

Garfield, B. (2006) Ain't gonna cover war no more. *On the Media*, 24 February. Available at http://www.onthemedia.org/transcripts/2006/02/24/04.

Garofoli, J. (2006) Cell phone videos of war let Internet viewers hear the rockets, feel the terror. *San Francisco Chronicle*, 28 July, A1.

Gellhorn, M. (1998) *The face of war*. London: Granta.

Gelzinis, P. (2003) Trying to understand a former colleague's lapse in judgment. *Boston Herald*, 3 April.

Geraci, C. (2004a) 'Seattle Times' regrets Silicio's firing, doesn't regret coffin photo. *Editor & Publisher*, 22 April.

Geraci, C. (2004b) Woman who took 'coffin' photo hails press coverage. *Editor & Publisher*, 28 April.

Gerth, J., and Shane, S. (2005) US is said to pay to plant articles in Iraqi papers. *New York Times*, 1 December. Available at http://www.nytimes.com/2005/12/01/politics/01propaganda.html?_r=1&oref=slogin.

Gibson, O. (2003) Spin caught in a web trap. *The Guardian*, 17 February, 34. Available at http://www.guardian.co.uk/media/2003/feb/17/mondaymediasection.Iraqandthemedia.

Gillan, A. (2007) MoD issues gag order on armed forces. *The Guardian*, 10 August.

GIPI-AF (2006) Promoting Internet policy and regulation reform in Afghanistan. Assessment report: State of telecommunications and

Internet in Afghanistan. *InterNews Europe*. December. Available at http://www.internews.fr/spip.php?article46.

Glaser, M. (2005) Did London bombings turn citizen journalists into citizen paparazzi? *Online Journalism Review*, 12 July. Available at http://www.ojr.org/ojr/stories/050712glaser/.

Goodman, A. (2008) Gareth Porter: Official version of US–Iranian naval incident starts to unravel [transcript]. *DemocracyNow!*, 11 January. Available at http://www.democracynow.org/2008/1/11/us_backs_off_claim_of_naval.

Goodman, E. (1999) The first Internet war. *Boston Globe*, 8 April.

Goodman, G. (1999) Too many truths. *British Journalism Review*, 10 (3).

Gottleib, J. (dir.) (2003) *CNN Presents: War in Iraq: The Road to Baghdad*. CNN.

Gowing, N. (2003) Journalists and war: The troubling new tensions post 9/11. In D. K. Thussu and D. Freedman (eds), *War and the media*. London: Sage, 231–40.

Gray, C. H. (1997) *Postmodern war: The new politics of conflict*. New York: Guilford Press.

Griffiths, M. (2003) e-Citizens: Blogging as democratic practice. *Electronic Journal of e-Government*, 2 (3). Available at http://www.ejeg.com/volume-2/volume2-issue3/v2-i3-art2.htm.

Guensburg, C. (1999) Online access to the war zone. *American Journalism Review*, 21 (4).

Haas, T. (2005) From 'public journalism' to the 'public's journalism'? Rhetoric and reality in the discourse on weblogs. *Journalism Studies*, 6 (3), 387–96.

Hallin, D. C. (1986) *The 'uncensored war': The media and Vietnam*. New York: Oxford University Press.

Hamilton, J. M., and Jenner, E. (2004) Redefining foreign correspondence. *Journalism*, 5 (3), 301–21.

Hammond, A. (2006) Outspoken Saudi bloggers wary of 'official' group. *Reuters Technology News*, 4 May.

Hammond, P. (2007) *Media, war, and postmodernity*. London and New York: Routledge.

Harmon, A. (2004) New technology loosens controls over images of war. *New York Times*, 14 May.

Harris, M. E. (2003) War photography: From the field to the cover. *Digital Photo Pro*, November/December.

Hassan, R. (2008) *The information society*. Cambridge: Polity.

Hebert, J. (2004) The art of blogging attracts a burgeoning number of fans. *San Diego Union-Tribune*, 18 July, 1–3.

Hedges, C. (1996) Serb's answer to oppression: Their web site. *New York Times*, 8 December.

Hedges, C. (2002) *War is a force that gives us meaning*, New York: PublicAffairs.

Heidt, M. (2004) SEALS ambush the AP this time. *Froggy Ruminations*, 28 December. Available at: http://froggyruminations.blogspot. com/2004_12_01_archive.html.

Helmore, E. (2007) Saddam's 'snuff video' signals the end of editorial control. *The Observer*, 7 January.

Hersh, S. (2004) Torture at Abu Ghraib. *New Yorker*, 10 May. Available at http://www.newyorker.com/archive/2004/05/10/040510fa_fact.

Hirsh, M. (1999) Casualties of war. *Newsweek*, 9 January.

Hockenberry, J. (2005) The blogs of war. *Wired*, 13 (8). Available at http://www.wired.com/wired/archive/13.08/milblogs_pr.html.

Hogge, B. (2007) Reporting Africa, blog by blog. *OpenDemocracy*, 28 February. Available at http://www.opendemocracy.net/media/africa_blog_4390.jsp.

Hoskins, A. (2004) *Televising war: From Vietnam to Iraq*. London: Continuum.

Howton, E. (1999) Kosovo teenager shares her plight through e-mail to Berkeley pen pal. *San Jose Mercury News*, 26 March.

Hull, D. (2004) The war on Iraq: A reporter's observations. In Y. R. Kamalipour and N. Snow (eds), *War, media and propaganda*. Oxford: Rowman & Littlefield, 131–7.

Hunter, D., and Werbach K. (2005) 10 questions with . . . Dan Hunter and Kevin Werbach on blogs and a new information center of gravity. *Journal of Financial Planning*, 18 (9), 10–18.

Ignatieff, M. (1999) *Virtual war*. New York: Vintage.

Irby, K. (2003) L. A. Times photographer fired over altered image. *PoynterOnline*, 2 April.

Jahn, G. (1999) Web site documents strikes as they occur. *The Star-Ledger*, 25 April.

Jeffords, S., and Rabinovitz, L. (eds) (1994) *Seeing through the media: The Persian Gulf War*. New Brunswick, NJ: Rutgers University Press.

Jenkins, H. (2006) *Convergence culture: Where old and new media collide*. New York: New York University Press.

JuliaAnn (2007) Those Iraqi bloggers sure write like Karen Hughes. *Daily Kos*, 28 March. Available at http://www.dailykos.com/storyonly/2007/3/29/0264/31213.

Jurkowitz, M. (2004) A war of images: The bombardment of brutal pictures from Iraq is making the conflict a reality for Americans. *Boston Globe*, 15 May, C1.

Kahney, L. (1999) Net dispatches from Kosovo's war. *Wired*, 26 March.

Kahney, L. (2001) Who said the Web fell apart? *Wired News*, 12 September. Available at http://www.wired.com/news/culture/0,1284,46766,00. html.

Kaldor, M. (2003) *Global civil society: An answer to war.* Cambridge: Polity.

Kaldor, M. (2006) *New & old wars.* 2nd edn, Cambridge: Polity.

Kamber, M., and Arango, T. (2008) 4,000 US deaths, and a handful of images. *New York Times*, 26 July.

Kanaley, R. (1999) War dispatches posted on internet. *Philadelphia Inquirer*, 27 March.

Katz, I. (2003) Introduction. In S. Pax (ed.), *The Baghdad blog.* London: Atlantic Books, ix–xiv.

Katz, J. (1999a) Did Monica obsession obscure smoldering Kosovo? *Freedom Forum*, 4 August.

Katz, J. (1999b) War coverage is not the Net's strength. *Freedom Forum*, 13 April.

Kavoori, A. P., and Fraley, T. (2006) *Media, terrorism, and theory: A reader.* Lanham, MD: Rowman & Littlefield.

Kawamoto, K. (ed.) (2003) *Digital journalism: Emerging media and the changing horizons of journalism.* Lanham, MD: Rowman & Littlefield.

Keeble, R. (1997) *Secret state, silent press.* Luton: John Libbey.

Keen, A. (2007) *The cult of the amateur: How today's internet is killing our culture.* New York: Doubleday/Currency.

Kellner, D. (2004) The Persian Gulf TV war revisited. In S. Allan and B. Zelizer (eds), *Reporting war: Journalism in wartime.* London and New York: Routledge, 136–54.

Kellner, D. (2005) *Media spectacle and the crisis of democracy: Terrorism, war, and election battles.* Boulder, CO, and London: Paradigm.

Kelly, P. (2004) The damage is done. *The Australian*, 8 May, 30.

Khan, S. (2008) Twitter cause a little controversy after Mumbai attacks: What about Pakistan? *Green & White*, 27 November. Available at http://greenwhite.org/author/skhan.

Khokhlova, V. (2008) Georgia, Russia: The war's virtual dimension. *Global Voices Online*, 16 August. Available at http://globalvoicesonline.org/2008/08/16/georgia-russia-the-wars-virtual-dimension/.

Kitfield, J. (1999) Command and control: the messenger. *National Journal*, 31, 11 September, 2546.

Kitfield, J. (2001) Lessons from Kosovo. *Media Studies Journal*, summer, 37–9.

Klopfenstein, B. (2006) Terrorism and the exploitation of new media. In A. P. Kavoori and T. Fraley (eds), *Media, terrorism and theory: A reader.* Lanham, MD: Rowman and Littlefield, 107–20.

Knightley, P. (1991) Here is the patriotically censored news. *Index on Censorship*, 20 (4/5), 4–5.

Knightley, P. (2004) *The first casualty: The war correspondent as hero and myth-maker from the Crimea to Iraq*. 3rd edn, Baltimore: Johns Hopkins University Press.

Komp, C. (2006) Witness to war. *Clamor*, 26 (spring).

Krikorian, O. (2008) Georgia: Blogging the war. *Global Voices Online*, 28 August. Available at http://globalvoicesonline.org/2008/08/28/georgia-blogging-the-war/.

Kurtz, H. (2003) Altered picture costs LA Times photographer his job. *Washington Post*, 3 April.

Kurtz, H. (2005) Eason Jordan, quote, unquote: CNN news chief clarifies his comments on Iraq. *Washington Post*, 8 February, C1. Available at http://www.washingtonpost.com/wp-dyn/articles/A6490-2005Feb7.html.

Lanson, J. (2003) War isn't pretty, nor is news of it. *Christian Science Monitor*, 25 March.

Lasica, J. D. (1999) Conveying the war in human terms. *American Journalism Review*, June, 76.

Leadbetter, C., and Miller, P. (2004) *The pro-am revolution: How enthusiasts are changing our economy and society*. Demos, 24 November. Available at http://www.demos.co.uk/files/proamrevolutionfinal.pdf.

Levinson, P. (2004) *Cellphone: The story of the world's most mobile medium and how it has transformed everything!*, New York: Palgrave Macmillan.

Levy, S. (2003) Blogger's delight. *Newsweek Web Exclusive*, 28 March.

Lewis, J. (2006) *Shoot first and ask questions later: Media coverage of the 2003 Iraq War*. New York: Peter Lang.

Linehan, H. (2005) Eveyone's a journalist now. *Irish Times*, 16 July, 3.

Littlefield, K. (1999) Growth of international news yields more options, more challenges. *Orange County Register*, 12 May.

Loyn, D. (2005) *Frontline: The true story of the British mavericks who changed the face of war reporting*. London: Michael Joseph.

Lyke, M. L. (2003) We're in the thick of it, knowing precious little: Aboard the USS Abraham Lincoln. *Seattle Post-Intelligencer*, 20 March. Available at http://seattlepi.nwsource.com/lincoln/journal/index.asp?startAt=142.

Maass, P. (2003) Salam Pax is real. *Slate*, 2 June. Available at http://slate.msn.com/id/2083847/.

McAuliffe, K. (1999) Kosovo: A special report. *Columbia Journalism Review*, May/June.

McCarthy, M. (2003) War photo doctored in field shows ease of technology. *Wall Street Journal*, 2 April.

McCarthy, R. (2003) Salam's story. *The Guardian*, 30 May. Available at http://www.guardian.co.uk/world/2003/may/30/iraq.digitalmedia.

McFarquhar, N. (2007) US State Dept joins Arab-blog dialogue to sway 'silent majority'. *International Herald Tribune*, 24 September, 2: 5.

McGirk, T. (2006) Collateral damage or civilian massacre in Haditha? *Time*, 19 March. Available at http://www.time.com/time/world/article/0,8599,1174649-1,00.html.

MacKinnon, R. (2004) Blogging North Korea. *Nieman Reports*, 58 (3), 103–6.

McLeary, P. (2008) Blogging the long war. *Columbia Journalism Review*, 46 (6), 36–41.

Malik, S. (2006) Fucking straight death metal. *Journal of Visual Culture*, 5, 107–12.

Malkin, M. (2007) The trial of Bilal Hussein. *Michellemalkin.com*, 9 December. Available at http://michellemalkin.com/2007/12/09/the-trial-of-bilal-hussein/.

Maltby, S., and Keeble, R. (eds) (2007) *Communicating war: Memory, media and military*. Cambridge: Cambridge Scholars Press.

Matheson, D. (2009) What the blogger knows. In Z. Papacharissi (ed.), *Journalism and citizenship: New agendas in communication*. New York: Routledge, pp. 151–65.

Matheson, D., and Allan, S. (2007) Truth in a war zone: The role of warblogs in Iraq. In S. Maltby and R. Keeble (eds), *Communicating war: Memory, media, military*. Cambridge: Cambridge Scholars Press, 75–89.

Matic, V. (1999) Letter from Belgrade. *The Guardian*, 5 April.

Megna, M. (2003) Embedded in technology. *Daily News*, 6 April.

Meyer, P. (2003) The LA Times fires a photographer. *ZoneZero*. Available at http://www.zonezero.com/magazine/articles/altered/altered.html.

Miller, D. (2004) *Tell me lies: Propaganda and media distortion in the attack on Iraq*. London: Pluto Press.

Mirzoeff, N. (2005) *Watching Babylon: The war in Iraq and global visual culture*. New York: Routledge.

Mitchell, B. (2003) Weblogs: A road back to basics. *Nieman Reports*, 57 (3), 65–8.

Moeller, S. D. (1989) *Shooting war: Photography and the American experience of combat*. New York: Basic Books.

Moeller, S. D. (2009) *Packaging terrorism*. Malden, MA: Wiley-Blackwell.

Morozov, E. (2008) Citizen war-reporter? The Caucasus test. *openDemocracy*, 18 August. Available at http://www.opendemocracy.net/article/citizen-war-reporter.

Naím, M. (2007) The YouTube effect. *Foreign Policy*, 158 (Jan/Feb), 104–5.

Nance, M. (2008) Bowling for Boghammers ... 2008 edition. *Small*

Wars Journal, 12 January. Available at http://smallwarsjournal.com/blog/2008/01/bowling-for-boghammars-2008-ed-1/.

Norris, P., Kern, M., and Just, M. R. (2003) *Framing terrorism: The news media, the government, and the public*. New York: Routledge.

North, D. (1999) Kosovo's 'cyber-monk' and his mailing list. *Salon*, 26 March.

Norton, Q. (2005) Bridge blogs give voice to the marginalised. *Irish Times*, 15 July, 7.

Nossek, H., Sreberny, A., and Sonwalkar, P. (2007) *Media and political violence*. Cresskill, NJ: Hampton Press.

NucleophilicAttack (2005) Comment: The true face of war. *Metafilter*, 23 September. Available at http://www.metafilter.com/45343/The-true-face-of-war.

O'Neill, B. (2004) A shunned story. *Press Gazette*, 27 May, 5.

Overington, C. (2004) Sacked for photo Americans weren't meant to see. *Sydney Morning Herald*, 23 April.

Paine, K. (2008) Reputation redux: Russia invades Georgia by land and by server. *PR News*, August, 25.

Palmer, J., and Fontan, V. (2007) Our ears and our eyes. *Journalism*, 8 (1), 5–24.

Palser, B. (2003) Online advances. *American Journalism Review*, 1 May, 40–5.

Papacharissi, Z. (2002) The virtual sphere: The Internet as a public sphere. *New Media & Society*, 4 (1), 9–27.

Parry, R. L. (2001) A village is destroyed. And America says nothing happened. *The Independent*, 4 December, 1.

Paterson, C. A., and Domingo, D. (2008) *Making online news: The ethnography of new media production*. New York: Peter Lang.

Payne, K. (2005) The media as an instrument of war. *Parameters*, spring, 81–93.

PBS (2004) Called to account: Secretary Rumsfeld. *Online NewsHour*, 7 May. Available at http://www.pbs.org/newshour/bb/military/jan-june04/rum_05-07.html.

PBS (2007) Stories from a small planet, News war episode IV. 27 March. Available at http://www.pbs.org/frontlineworld/stories/newswar/.

PEJ (Project for Excellence in Journalism) (2003) Embedded reporters: What are Americans getting? Impressions: The potentials and risks of embedded reporting. 3 April. Available at http://www.journalism.org/node/213.

PEJ (Project for Excellence in Journalism) (2005) The state of the news media: An annual report on American journalism: Cable TV. Available at http://www.stateofthenewsmedia.com/2004/.

Pick, M., and Good, R. (2006) Iraq news: Bloggers and independent journalists are the only reliable sources for Western media news (before they are censored). *Robin Good's MasterNewMedia*, 23 December. Available at http://www.masternewmedia.org/news/2006/12/23/iraq_news_bloggers_and_independent.htm.

Pickerill, J., and Webster, F. (2006) The anti-war/peace movement in Britain and the conditions of information war. *International Relations*, 20 (4), 407–23.

PMI (Public Multimedia Inc.) (2007) Welcome page. Available at http://www.publicmultimedia.org/index.html.

Pounder, G. (2000) Opportunity lost. *Aerospace Power Journal*, summer, 56–78.

Rafeeq, A. (2007) Covering conflicts: The coverage of Iraq War II by the *New Zealand Herald*, the *Dominion Post* and *The Press*. PhD thesis, University of Canterbury, Christchurch.

Rai, P. (2007) Myanmar: Soldiers back down in Mandalay. *Global Voices Online*, 28 September. Available at http://www.globalvoicesonline.org/2007/09/28/myanmar-soldiers-back-down-in-mandalay/.

Raimondo, J. (1999) Allied farce: A wartime diary: A sight for sore eyes. *Antiwar.com*, 26 March. Available at http://www.antiwar.com/justin/?articleid=777.

Rainie, L., Fox, S., and Fallows, D. (2003) The Internet and the Iraq War: How online Americans have used the Internet to learn war news, understand events, and promote their views. *Pew Internet and American Life Project*, 1 April. Available at http://www.pewinternet.org/PPF/r/87/report_display.asp.

Reese, S. D. (2004) Militarized journalism: Framing dissent in the Gulf Wars. In S. Allan and B. Zelizer (eds), *Reporting war: Journalism in wartime*. London and New York: Routledge, 247–65.

Regan, T. (1999) Covering conflict on the World Wide Web. *Christian Science Monitor*, 29 April.

Regan, T. (2003) Weblogs threaten and inform traditional journalism. *Nieman Reports*, fall, 68–70.

Reid, C. (2007) Remembering David Bloom. MSNBC, 19 March. Available at http://video.msn.com/v/us/fv/msnbc/fv.htm??g=f6067f61-9cae-4934-99d9-cofa1e83d51a&f=00&fg=copy.

Rheingold, H. (2002) *Smart mobs: The next social revolution*. Cambridge, MA: Perseus.

Ricchiardi, S. (1999) Cracking down on Western journalists. *American Journalism Review*, May.

Ritchin, F. (2004) Photography's 'amateur hour'. *PixelPress.org*. Available at http://www.pixelpress.org/contents/essays_fs.html.

Rivera, R. (2004) Images of war dead a sensitive subject. *Seattle Times*, 22 April.

Riverbend (2004) Just go . . . *Baghdad Burning*, 7 May. Available at http://riverbendblog.blogspot.com/2004_05_01_riverbendblog_archive.html.

Roasa, D. (2008) Blogging the coup. *Columbia Journalism Review*, 46 (6), 12.

Rogers, S. (1999) The first web war. *The Guardian*, 26 March.

Rogerson, S. (2007) Information and integrity in the information age. *Ethical Space*, 4 (1–2), 10–12.

Roggio, B. (2006) Al-Zawraa: Muj TV. *Long War Journal*, 10 December. Available at http://billroggio.com/archives/2006/12/muj_tv.php.

Rorty, R. (1991) *Objectivity, relativism, and truth*. Cambridge and New York: Cambridge University Press.

Rosen, J. (2005) Eason Jordan resigns. *Pressthink*, 11 February. Available at http://journalism.nyu.edu/pubzone/weblogs/pressthink/2005/02/11/esn_res.html.

Rosen, J. (2006) The people formerly known as the audience. *Pressthink*, 27 June. Available at http://journalism.nyu.edu/pubzone/weblogs/pressthink/2006/06/27/ppl_frmr.html.

RSF (2007) Worldwide Press Freedom Index. *Reporters sans frontières*. Available at http://www.rsf.org/article.php3?id_article=24025.

RSF (2008) Three years of slaughter in Iraq. *Reporters sans frontières*. Available at http://www.rsf.org/special_iraq_en.php3.

Russell, A. (2001) Chiapas and the new news: Internet and newspaper coverage of a broken cease-fire. *Journalism*, 2, 197–220.

Rutten, T. (2003) Response to scandals validates credibility. *Los Angeles Times*, 7 May.

Sambrook, R. (2005) Citizen journalism and the BBC. *Nieman Reports*, 59 (4), 12–15.

Sava, H. (1999) Letter (republished). *National Post* [Canada], 31 March.

Schachtman, N. (2008) Military report: Secretly 'recruit or hire bloggers', Danger Room blog. *Wired*, 31 March. Available at http://blog.wired.com/defense/2008/03/report-recruit.html.

Schonfeld, R. (2007) Assignment Iraq: Letters. *Columbia Journalism Review*, 45 (5), 3–4.

Schreiner, M. (1999) Crisis over Kosovo. *Morning Star* [Wilmington, NC], 6 April.

Schuh, T. (2005) Faking the case against Syria. *Counterpunch*, 18 November. Available at http://www.counterpunch.org/schuh11182005.html.

Schulman, D. (2006) Mind games. *Columbia Journalism Review*, 45 (1), 38–44.

Schwab, N. (2007) Blogs chronicle war from soldiers' perspectives. *Washington Post*, 2 May. Available at http://www.washingtonpost.com/wp-dyn/content/article/2007/05/02/AR2007050202253_pf.html.

Scott, B. (2005) A contemporary history of digital journalism. *Television and New Media*, 6 (1), 89–126.

Seaton, J. (2005) *Carnage and the media: The making and breaking of news about violence*. London and New York: Allen Lane.

Seib, P. M. (2001) *Going live: Getting the news right in a real-time, online world*. Lanham, MD: Rowman & Littlefield.

Seib, P. (2003) Weaving the web: The Internet's effect on international news coverage and international relations. *Millennium: Journal of International Studies*, 32 (3), 617–41.

Seib, P. M. (2004) *Beyond the front lines: How the news media cover a world shaped by war*. New York: Palgrave Macmillan.

Sengupta, K. (2002) Saddam weaker now than before Gulf War, says report. *The Independent*, 10 September. Available at http://www.independent.co.uk/news/world/politics/saddam-weaker-now-than-before-gulf-war-says-report-607199.html.

Shane, S. (2005) Vietnam War intelligence 'deliberately skewed', secret study says. *New York Times*, 2 December, 11.

Shen, A. (2006) Tune in: 'Alive in Baghdad'. *Iraqslogger.com*, 22 December. Available at http://www.iraqslogger.com/index.php/post/284.

Silverstein, K. (2007) How the Pentagon's 'surrogates operation' feeds stories to administration-friendly media and pundits. *Harper's Magazine*, 13 August. Available at http://harpers.org/archive/2007/07/hbc-90000587.

Simon, E. (2004) Digital cameras change perception of war. MSNBC, 27 September. Available at http://www.msnbc.msn.com/id/6115600/.

Simpson, J. (2002) *News from no man's land: Reporting the world*. London: Macmillan.

Simpson, J. (2006) Saddam hanging taunts evoke ugly past. *BBC News Online*, 31 December. Available at http://news.bbc.co.uk/1/hi/world/middle_east/6221751.stm.

Sites, K. (2007) *In the hot zone*. New York: Harper.

Sliwinski, S. (2006) Camera war, again. *Journal of Visual Culture*, 5, 89–93.

Smith, V. (2007) Owning up to war. *From the frontline*, 1 (18), 5.

Snow, T. (2007) White House press secretary, Tony Snow, plugs LiveLeak. *LiveLeak*, 10 January. Available at http://www.liveleak.com/view?i=829607785c.

Sokwanele (2007) Talkin' about a revolution. *Sokwanele.com*, 23 March. Available at http://www.sokwanele.com/articles/sokwanele/talkinabout arevolution_23march2007.html.

Sontag, S. (2003) *Regarding the pain of others*. New York: Farrar, Straus and Giroux.

Sontag, S. (2004) Regarding the torture of others. *New York Times*, 23 May. Available at http://www.nytimes.com/2004/05/23/magazine/23PRISONS.html?ex=1400644800&en=a2cb6ea6bd297c8f&ei=5007&partner=USERLAND.

Sourcewatch (2008) Bloggers' roundtable. *Sourcewatch*, 22 April, 2008. Available at http://www.sourcewatch.org/index.php?title=Bloggers'_Roundtable.

Sulikova, S. V., and Perlmutter, D. D. (2007) Blogging down the dictator? The Kyrgyz revolution and *samizdat* websites. *International Communication Gazette*, 69 (1), 29–50.

Sullivan, K. (2006) E-mail, blogs, text messages propel anger over images: In hours, rumors in Denmark galvanize opinion elsewhere. *Washington Post*, 9 February, A14.

Swartz, J. (1999) Internet coverage defies media blackout. *San Francisco Chronicle*, 27 March.

Swartz, J. (2003) Iraq war could herald a new age of web-based news coverage. *USA Today*, 18 March. Available at http://www.usatoday.com/tech/news/2003-03-18-iraq-internet_x.htm.

Swofford, A. (2005) Gottfried talks only of hell: From the killing fields of Iraq: Four voices. *Columbia Journalism Review*, 44 (4), 60–5. Available at http://proquest.umi.com/pqdweb?did=939658371&sid=2&Fmt=1&clientId=13346&RQT=309&VName=PQD.

Sylvester, J. L., and Huffman, S. (eds) (2005) *Reporting from the front: The media and the military*. Lanham, MD: Rowman & Littlefield.

Taylor, P. M. (1992) *War and the media: Propaganda and persuasion in the Gulf War*. Manchester: Manchester University Press.

Thurman, N. (2007) The globalization of journalism online: A transatlantic study of news websites and their international readers. *Journalism*, 8 (3), 285–307.

Thussu, D. K. (2003) Live TV and bloodless deaths: war, infotainment and 24/7 news. In D. K. Thussu and D. Freedman (eds), *War and the media*. London: Sage, 117–32.

Tisdall, S., MacAskill, E., and Norton-Taylor, R. (2006) Special report: America's Long War. *The Guardian*, 15 February. Available at http://www.guardian.co.uk/world/2006/feb/15/politics.topstories3.

Tumber, H., and Palmer, J. (2004) *Media at war: The Iraq crisis*. London: Sage.

Tumber, H., and Webster, F. (2006) *Journalists under fire: Information war and journalistic practices*. London: Sage.

Umansky, E. (2006) Failures of imagination. *Columbia Journalism Review*, 45 (3), 16–31.

Van Riper, F. (2003) Manipulating truth, losing credibility. *Camera Works*, 9 April.

de Villepin, D. (2003) Address by Dominique de Villepin, French minister of foreign affairs, before the United Nations Security Council. United Nations, 19 March. Available at http://www.un.int/france/documents_anglais/030319_cs_villepin_irak.htm.

Virilio, P. (1989) *War and cinema: The logistics of perception*. London and New York: Verso.

Virilio, P. (1994) *The Vision Machine*, trans. J. Rose. Bloomington: Indiana University Press.

Vujakovic, P. (2002) Mapping the war zone: Cartography, geopolitics and security discourse in the UK press. *Journalism Studies*, 3 (2), 187–202.

Wall, M. (2005) Blogging Gulf War II. *Journalism Studies*, 7 (1), 111–26.

Walsh, L., and Barbara, J. (2006) Speed, international security, and 'new war' coverage in cyberspace. *Journal of Computer-Mediated Communication*, 12 (1).

Walski, B. (2003) Brian Walski discusses his doctored photo: Interview with David Walker. *Photo District News*, 7 May.

Wark, M. (1994) Vectoral perception and cultural studies. *Journal of International Communication*, 1 (1), 60–87.

Wasserman, E. (2001) The videophone war. *American Journalism Review*, 1 (November), 22.

Wellman, B., Quan-Haase, A., Boase, J., Chen, W., Hampton, K., Isla de Diaz, I., and Miyata, K. (2003) The social affordances of the internet for networked individualism. *Journal of Computer-Mediated Communication* 8 (3). Available at http://www.ascusc.org/jcmc/vol8/issue3/wellman.html.

Wilby, P. (2008) Georgia has won the PR war. *MediaGuardian*, 18 August, 7.

Williams, R. (1982) Distance. In A. O'Connor (ed.), *Raymond Williams on Television*. London: Routledge.

Williams, R. ([1958] 1989) Culture is ordinary. In R. Gable (ed.), *Resources of Hope*. London: Verso.

Wired (2008) Fallujah mosque shooting. Wired channel, *YouTube*, 21 April. Available at http://www.youtube.com/watch?v=04j5oghDeKA.

Woodward, R. B. (2007) Subtext message. *Wall Street Journal*, 4 January.

Wright, R. (2004) Technology changing how we see war: Up close. *Los Angeles Times*, 23 May.

Zelizer, B. (2002) Photography, journalism and trauma, In B. Zelizer and S. Allan (eds), *Journalism after September 11*. London and New York: Routledge, 48–68.

Zelizer, B. (2005) Death in wartime: Photographs and the 'other war' in Afghanistan. *Harvard International Journal of Press Politics*, 10 (3), 26–55.

Zelizer, B. (2007) On 'having been there': 'Eyewitnessing' as a journalistic key word. *Critical Studies in Media Communication*, 24 (5), 408–28.

Zelizer, B., and Allan, S. (eds) (2002) *Journalism after September 11*. London and New York: Routledge.

Zremski, J. (2004) Fighting for survival: Violent downward spiral leaves many on the front lines wondering if Iraq can ever recover. *Buffalo News*, 24 October, H1.

Zuckerman, E. (2008) The cute cat theory talk at ETech. My heart's in Accra [blog], 8 March. Available at http://www.ethanzuckerman.com/blog/2008/03/08/the-cute-cat-theory-talk-at-etech/.

Index

Page numbers followed by '*p*' refer to a photograph.